☆ ☆ ☆ | # JOHN QUINCY ADAMS

BY THE SAME AUTHOR

JOHN QUINCY ADAMS

☆ ☆ ☆ ☆ ☆ ☆

A Biography of
The Sixth President of
The United States

by EDWIN P. HOYT

REILLY & LEE CO.
Chicago · 1963

*For Aunt Marion and
Uncle Dick, who understand
the impact of the land
upon the man.*

TABLE OF CONTENTS

☆ ☆ ☆

CHAPTER 1

Child of Revolution

In a republic seldom has a man grown from boyhood to adult maturity with a great destiny foreshadowed. There is no established political succession in a republic, similar to royal succession in a monarchy, and it has been an American boast that every youth could aspire to become President of the United States. If that boast has never been exactly truthful, at least it has been more truthful here than in any other republic. Even though a favored group has existed in the American nation since before it was a nation, it has always been possible for men of ability to break through the crust of privilege. And in a sense this important characteristic of the American system began in the mature days of John Quincy Adams, who was to be sixth President of the United States.

If there was ever an American youth who was marked from boyhood with the potential of greatness it was John Quincy Adams. From his eleventh year he rubbed shoulders with the leaders of nations. He conversed with Thomas Jefferson and Benjamin Franklin, and listened to their conversations with his father. He mingled with the courtiers and intellectuals of the French court. He traveled widely in days when travel was the privilege of the very wealthy, and when there was no better way to learn about the world around him. He was intimate with many of the little group of leaders who established the American republic. As much

as it could be said of any man, it could be said that John
Quincy Adams was the logical successor to James Monroe
as President of the United States in 1824. It had been generally accepted in governing circles that the path to the
Presidency lay through the office of Secretary of State.
Adams held that office under Monroe. He did become President of the United States, as expected. But therewith, all
the scarcely established traditions about the American Presidency collapsed. For John Quincy Adams' tenure in office
was not a happy one, and even as he served out his first term
it was apparent that there would be no second term.

Partly, it was the character of the man himeslf that made
this change so certain. Partly it was the changing character
of America. And was that change for better or for worse?
The answer lies in the historical fact that after Adams had
been defeated for a second term in the nation's highest
office, the former President sought and won election to the
House of Representatives. In that important office he served
out the rest of his life with distinction and honor. In effect,
John Quincy Adams enjoyed a second public career. It was
proof of his great abilities. It was also proof of the stability
of the young American nation, for here a man who had
wielded great power in high office was safe from his enemies
after the power was lost. In the first half of the nineteenth
century, such a statement could not be made about many
nations of the world.

John Quincy Adams was born on July 11, 1767 in the
North Parish of Braintree, Massachusetts colony, which
was later to be incorporated in the town of Quincy. He
came, on both sides, from local families. The first Adams
had come to the Bay Colony sometime before 1640, to settle
in Braintree and run a farm. His father's family had been
farmers until John Adams took to the law, to become both
farmer and lawyer. His mother, Abigail Adams, was the

daughter of William Smith, a minister in the community of Weymouth, and, as such, one of the most respected men in a colony which had been founded by religious men.

John Adams had inherited his farm from his father some six years before the birth of John Quincy Adams. He had grown up on that same farm, located at the foot of Penn's Hill, and he had ridden his own mare off from the farm to Cambridge to attend Harvard College. After college and study of the law, John Adams had rapidly built a flourishing practice among the merchants of Boston. And as a man concerned with the law, John Adams had been equally concerned with the inequities heaped upon the American colonies by Great Britain.

Twelve days before the birth of John Quincy Adams, in far-off London, Chancellor of the Exchequer Charles Townshend secured the King's assent to a new series of tax laws that affected America. These laws established a new set of import duties on products brought into the colonies: on glass, paints, and tea, among other goods. The new taxes aroused a fever of resentment in the colonies, and were to be known with passion as the hated Townshend Acts, the successors to the Stamp Act, which had been repealed when the colonists fought against it.

John Quincy Adams, born on the family farm, was named for his father and his great-grandfather, John Quincy, who had represented the town of Braintree in the colonial legislature of Massachusetts for forty years. Old John Quincy was Speaker of that House for many of those years. He was dying as the son of John Adams was born, and the boy received the old man's name.

A year afterwards, the John Adams family was living in Boston. Adams felt this move was necessary if he were to pursue his law practice. For now, the legal profession had become most important to John Adams. As a lawyer who rode the circuits to appear before His Majesty's colonial judges, Adams had an opportunity to become well aware of the growing sentiment against the oppressive taxes.

The Americans banded together secretly and began to harass their British overlords. They refused to import English goods. They published secret newspapers which attacked British rule. They rose in violence against British law. Britain's government replied by sending British troops to Boston, the center of the activity of the rebellious colonists. For nearly a year and a half the troops were quartered there, causing excitement and anger.

In March, 1770, a soldier and a worker were involved in a fist fight, and an angry crowd of colonists interfered. That night colonists and soldiers were both ready for trouble— and it came. A sentry near the State House was troubled by a gang, and he called the main guard to his assistance. The guard arrived and fired into the crowd. In the end, five men were dead or dying. Public feeling ran so high that the British troops were withdrawn from Boston to islands in Boston harbor.

The captain of the guard and six soldiers were tried for murder. Their defenders were John Adams and Josiah Quincy, both able attorneys and both known as American patriots. When the case was over, the captain and four soldiers were acquitted, and two soldiers were branded on the hand. One might suspect that John Adams would have grown unpopular after this court case, but the reverse was true. He was appointed to the Massachusetts legislature and there renewed his interest in the cause of colonial freedom.

The rebellion grew, and John Adams was in the thick of it from the time of the Boston Tea Party of 1773. When the British increased their restrictive measures, the Massachusetts legislature appointed delegates to attend a Continental Congress in Philadelphia. John Adams was one of those selected.

Thereafter, for nearly four years, the boy John Quincy Adams saw little of his father. When he was eight years old a company of militia stopped at the Adams farm overnight, on their trip to Lexington. Before the soldiers, young John Quincy Adams stood up with a musket that seemed as big as a cannon, and went through the manual of arms.

The boy and his mother remained at the family farm in Braintree along with his elder sister. They lived in constant fear that they would be raided or imprisoned by British soldiers, since John Adams was one of the ringleaders of the revolutionaries. On June 17, 1775, Abigail Adams took her son by the hand and led him up Penn's hill when the crash of cannon drifted across the farmland from distant Bunker Hill. The boy and his mother listened to the battle and watched the smoke drift along the bay from fires in Charlestown.

When they returned home, they learned the price of war. News arrived that Dr. Joseph Warren, the family physician, had been killed in this struggle. It seemed only a few hours before that the doctor had been with the family, setting the broken forefinger of the boy. War was not just gunfire and shouting, John Quincy Adams realized. It meant death.

Death did not frighten John Quincy Adams as much as it might have frightened other boys in other times. From his mother, John learned two sets of principles. He was taught to study and honor the Bible, in the faith of the Congregationalists of Braintree. But Abigail Adams also taught her son an ode to patriot warriors who had fallen in the last effort of the Stuart kings to seize control of England in 1745, the war called the second Jacobite Rebellion. All the rest of his life, John Quincy Adams was to say the Lord's Prayer every morning before arising, and then recite this ode to fallen warriors.

When John was ten years old, he undertook a job for his mother that she would never have asked in times of peace.

He became the family "post rider," delivering and collecting the Adams mail at Boston, nine miles away from the Braintree farm. He was a responsible member of the family at an age when most boys are still playing with lead soldiers.

The education of John Quincy Adams in these years was directed almost entirely by his mother. The town had closed the grammar school to save money for the war against the British, and the schoolteacher had gone off to serve in the army. But John Quincy Adams learned to read and write before he was old enough to work on the farm. When he was ten years old he was reading Shakespeare and trying to read John Milton's *Paradise Lost*.

At this time, John Quincy Adams was studying with his father's law clerk, John Thaxter. He read Greek and Latin under Thaxter and became proficient enough in both to continue his studies later. If it was a disordered education, at least it was vigorously pursued. In view of the condition of the colonies at the beginning, and the condition of the states in the middle of the revolution, it was a very wholesome education.

Two years after the Declaration of Independence, John Adams became discouraged with the lack of progress of the revolution and with his own efforts in the Continental Congress in Philadelphia. He came home, released by his friends in the government, to try to live a more normal existence. He began, once again, to practice law and to take over the operation of his farm. He was on leave of absence, to be sure, but he did not expect to be called back to government again soon.

But in the beginning of 1778, John Adams was appointed by Congress to travel to France, and there to join Benjamin Franklin in trying to persuade Louis XVI to assist the infant United States in the struggle against England. Adams accepted the appointment, and took with him on his voyage his son, John Quincy, and two other small boys. On February 13, 1778, John Quincy Adams and the others stepped into a ship's boat before his uncle Norton Quincy's home on the rocky shore of Braintree. They were bundled in coarse blankets, and they sank their feet deep in the hay piled in the boat to protect them from the wintry winds. Sailors of the new American navy rowed the diplomatic party out to the Frigate *Boston,* which lay at anchor in the harbor, and the voyage to France began.

The winter voyage across the Atlantic Ocean was dreadful. Almost as soon as the *Boston* raised anchor, she was sighted by a British squadron which pursued the ship for two days. The British ships had scarcely sunk below the horizon when a frightening storm threatened the little wooden ship and sent passengers and crew into violent spasms of seasickness. One night, during the height of the storm, a bolt of lightning struck one of the masts of the ship, injuring more than a score of members of the crew.

The *Boston* emerged from the storm, still relatively sound, to discover the presence of a British privateer in the area. Captain Samuel Parker had been ordered to deliver John Adams to France; that was the purpose of the voyage. He wanted to engage the privateer, but Adams had the power of decision, for his safety was more important to the infant American government than the capture of a prize of war. John Adams agreed that it would be good to capture the British ship, however, and allowed Parker to go into battle.

It was a battle, too. There was no mistake about that. Young John Quincy Adams stood on the deck below the main, eyes glued against a porthole, trying to see what he could of the action. A cannonball whizzed by the head of his father, on the deck above, carrying away a heavy boom. But then the frigate fired her broadside, and the lightly-armed privateer had no choice but to strike her colors and surrender to the heavier American ship. A prize crew was detached from the *Boston* and the captured ship was sent back to the United States.

Not long afterward, the first lieutenant of the *Boston* was injured when a signal gun exploded. John Adams held the officer in his arms while the ship's surgeon amputated. Indeed, ten-year-old John Quincy Adams was receiving a rich, practical education.

On the voyage the boy's father and several French gentlemen aboard tried to instruct the young travelers in French. But the boys learned far more rapidly once the ship had docked at Bordeaux, and they found it necessary to order their dinners in a foreign tongue.

The Adamses, father and son, went to stay with Benjamin Franklin in his house at Passy, a suburb of Paris. After a few days of sightseeing, John Quincy Adams entered a formal school, in the company of two of Franklin's grandsons. The boys boarded at the school, studying French and Latin, and learning music, drawing, dancing, and the far more exciting art of fencing. They were being given the kind of education prescribed for young gentlemen in Europe in that period.

John Adams and his wife Abigail had strong senses of history. They knew they were participating in the development of a new nation, and they felt certain that their son John Quincy Adams would one day take a place as one of the leaders of that nation. John Adams advised his son to maintain a diary, which the boy began to do. His mother, at home in Braintree, wrote him to remind him to mind his morals and his manners, which he did not fail to do. Together, the parents gave John Quincy Adams, even at the age of eleven, a sense of importance and responsibility which he was never to lose.

In one of his earliest letters to his mother, he noted that

he had been to see the Palace and gardens at Versailles, the
military school at Paris, several hospitals, the cathedral of
Notre Dame, and that he had wandered through a number
of areas of Paris, including Montmartre. He also noted,
ruefully, that he had neglected to make notes about these
trips, and promised to do better in the future.

He was a dutiful son, and perhaps wise beyond his years.
"A journal book and a letter book of a lad of eleven years
old can not be expected to contain much of science, litera-
ture, arts, wisdom, or wit," he wrote, "yet it may serve to
perpetuate many observations that I may make, and may
hereafter help me to recollect both persons and things that
would otherwise escape my memory."

Yet, John Quincy Adams was a boy, first of all. The
months passed, and his good intentions about keeping a
journal fell by the wayside. There was too much to be done.
On Sundays he followed the French custom and went to
Mass at the Church of the Minimes near the school. He
attended the Théâtre des Petits Comédiens, where a group
of children gave performances in the Bois de Boulogne, and
he acquired a taste for the theater. He quarreled with the
other American boys, played with them, and studied with
them. If the journal languished, it was not because John
Quincy Adams was lazy, but because he had a very great
deal to occupy his mind.

John Adams had scarcely arrived in Paris when it became
apparent that there was little real need for his services. The
French government had concluded treaties of commerce
and friendship with the fledgling American republic. There
was certainly need for a minister from the United States to
France, but not for a whole commission of ministers.

The appointment as Minister to France was given to
Benjamin Franklin. Thereupon, without any further word
from the Congress in Philadelphia as to what was expected

of him, John Adams decided to go home and to take his son with him.

The trip was delayed when His Majesty's government announced that it would be delighted to give Mr. Adams passage on the French Frigate *Sensible,* which would also carry the first French Minister to America on his voyage to the post. Diplomatically speaking, it was impossible to refuse the offer, no matter what plans had been made. John Quincy Adams learned of the demands of diplomacy in that affair, for the impatient John Adams and his son were forced to remain in France for many weeks, awaiting the pleasure of the French government.

Finally, three months after the Adamses had hoped to leave, the *Sensible* was ready, and so was the Chevalier de la Luzerne, France's first Minister to America. Aboard ship the French and American Ministers mingled freely. John Quincy Adams, in fact, earned the gratitude of the French Minister by helping him to learn the English he would need in his new post.

John Adams and his son arrived in Boston on August 2, 1779, having been away from home for a year and a half. John Quincy Adams hoped now to be sent to Andover Academy, to polish his Greek and Latin, and the other subjects which would make it possible for him to enter Harvard college. But his father and mother had other ideas. His mother told him one day that it would be far better for his education to return to France with his father than to spend a year or two in Andover Academy.

Return to France? Yes, his father had been appointed Minister Plenipotentiary to negotiate a peace with England. The appointment was made within weeks of the return of the two Adamses from the first European trip. The war was not nearly over, it would not end for three more years, but the French Foreign Minister believed it was important that the United States keep an ambassador in Europe who would be ready to negotiate for peace at any moment. Congress chose John Adams for that post.

John Quincy Adams was reluctant but he was also an obedient son who accepted without complaint the future his father and mother mapped so carefully for him.

He put aside his hopes of an American education and asked his father to take him along once again—this time with his younger brother Charles.

The ship on which they traveled to Europe was the same vessel on which they had come home—the French Frigate *Sensible*. But where the voyage home had been quiet, the voyage to Europe was again as frightening as the first trip on the *Boston*. Far out in the currents of the Atlantic ocean, the *Sensible* encountered the Atlantic's autumn storms, and developed a hole in her wooden bottom that John Quincy Adams said was as large "as a man's head"—or so the captain said. The crew worked the pumps, but the captain became concerned enough about the safety of his ship that he put in at the port of Ferrol, Spain, and the passengers disembarked there. The group landed a week before Christmas in 1779. After the holidays, it became apparent that the ship would be in port for a long time before she could proceed. So the Adams family and others of the party made their way painfully over the mountains of northern Spain and into southern France—a journey by foot and mule and creaking cart that added much to the education of John Quincy Adams. Finally the party reached Paris, and there the Adams boys were placed in John Quincy's old school at Passy, the school of M. le Coeur, where they went back to lessons in fencing and dancing and the classics.

While he was waiting to represent the American republic in peace negotiations, John Adams was called upon by the Congress to seek financial assistance for the United States from the Dutch government. The Adams family, then, moved on to Amsterdam, where the father represented his government to that of the Netherlands. The two boys entered the public Latin School at Amsterdam, but Charles was growing so homesick that his father took pity on him and sent him back to the United States to rejoin his mother and sister. John Quincy Adams displayed none of that homesickness, but he became thoroughly sick of the Latin School which was conducted arbitrarily and harshly by its masters. After four months in that school he persuaded his father to allow him to attend the University of Leyden, and there he went to school for five months, learning Dutch as well as the classics that would be required of him if he wished to continue his formal education.

It did not seem likely that John Quincy Adams would follow such a course, at least not in the summer of 1781. That July, Francis Dana, an old friend of the Adams family, was selected by Congress to travel to Russia to try to persuade Catherine the Great to recognize the new American government. Dana needed a secretary, someone who could speak and read French fluently and could copy official letters. John Adams suggested that his son could do this, and thus the fourteen-year-old boy became secretary to the new Minister. On July 7, 1781, the party set out for St. Petersburg from Amsterdam. Dana and John Quincy Adams did not arrive until August 29—so long did it take to travel across Europe and Russia in those days.

Minister Dana's mission met with no success, but John Quincy Adams learned some of the mysteries of world affairs and human conduct in the fourteen months he spent in the Russian capital. Young Adams continued his studies alone, working on his Greek and Latin, and reading heavily in history, since Commissioner Dana subscribed to an English-language library in St. Petersburg.

After fourteen months, when it was apparent that Dana would not leave Russia at least until the following spring, John Quincy Adams wanted to go back to the Hague to join his father. In the company of an Italian nobleman he set out in the autumn, even though winter had already closed in on St. Petersburg. Six weeks later they arrived in Stockholm, where John Quincy Adams remained for a number of weeks. He traveled to Copenhagen and then to Hamburg, but so slow was the journey that it was April 20, 1783 when young Adams returned to his father's house in the Hague.

Old John Adams had been busy. He had traveled to Europe this second time at the suggestion of the Comte de Vergennes, the French foreign minister. But in the years since the beginning of the revolution, the French had tired of the struggle, and would have been ready to settle, on behalf of the Americans, for less than the whole loaf of freedom. John Adams resisted this trend in every possible way. He pushed and pulled and was largely instrumental in the huge victory the tiny American republic won at the bargaining table. It was this victory which made it possible for the United States to eventually become a nation that extended from the Atlantic to the Pacific ocean. Had the treaty been worked out in another way, as was proposed, the nation could never have expanded so far west, and thus could never have become as homogeneous and powerful as it did become. John Quincy Adams did not learn much of the details of the peace negotiation until many years later, but he knew enough to be proud of his father and to understand that his father had carried the torch of freedom high.

Although John Quincy Adams was only 15 years old in 1783, he had already done much. He had traveled twice across the Atlantic, once experiencing an actual naval battle. He had been nearly shipwrecked in a storm, and had worried with the captain and crew in a leaky ship floundering for port. He had attended the theater often (and even fallen in love from afar with an actress). He had traveled as secretary and interpreter across Europe. He had been given an insight into the most confidential dispatches and matters of state. He had observed king and queens in their courts. He had attended many different kinds of religious services. He had learned at least smatterings of half a dozen languages, and had acquired a perfect command of French, the language of diplomacy, so-called because it was the one language all diplomats spoke in common.

John Quincy Adams had learned all these graces and subjects with only three years of formal schooling, but so effective was his education that he was able to undertake a long overland voyage, as that from St. Petersburg, without serious fear.

Obviously, at fifteen, John Quincy Adams was an educated youth, with a very special kind of education that in some ways transcended that of his elders, even of his father and such men as Thomas Jefferson. John Quincy was not ready to step into the shoes of any of these founders of the Republic, nor had he any illusions about his own educational failings. But his progress was impressive indeed.

The father saw the potential in his son, and instead of sending him back to school, allowed John Quincy Adams to become an extra secretary with the American delegation which now moved back to Paris to negotiate treaties of friendship with various nations. Thomas Jefferson, Benjamin Franklin and the elder Adams made up the commission. As his father's secretary, John Quincy Adams came into frequent contact with Jefferson, whom he particularly admired and called a "man of universal learning," not realizing how firm a foundation he had already laid for his own career—at least in the field of national government.

For two years John Quincy Adams remained in Europe, mostly in Paris. He traveled to England occasionally, and elsewhere on the continent. His mother and sister came to England to join the family's men.

It was agreed, however, between father and son that the son would leave Europe one day to return home and attend Harvard College. John Adams gave up many of his evenings to that end, teaching his son algebra, geometry, and even trigonometry to prepare the boy for the requirements of the college.

In the springtime of 1785, John Quincy Adams did return to America. It was a wrench. Up until a few months beforehand, although he had been making his plans to return, John Quincy Adams was not certain that he would do so. When his father was appointed the first minister to Great Britain, the temptation to remain with the family was great, but young Adams firmly put it aside, and set sail for America. Why? For one reason because young Adams was shrewdly conscious of the situation of his own family. In his diary, he wrote:

"My father has been so much taken up all his lifetime with the interests of the public, that his own fortune has suffered by it; so that his children will have to provide for themselves, which I shall never be able to do, if I loiter away my precious time in Europe and shun going home until I am forced to it."

By going home, John Quincy Adams would again build ties with an America that seemed strange to him, and he knew this to be important. When he arrived in Boston, he decided that he had not enough education, so he spent several months studying Latin and Greek at the home of a relative. In the spring of 1786, he was given an examination by the President of Harvard, but it was not a very searching one. The college was so pleased to welcome the son of the

American Ambassador to London that he was not charged
tuition fees.

Young Adams spent less than two years in Harvard College
and graduated with honors in the spring of 1787. He was
second in his class and was honored by being chosen to make
an oration at the commencement exercise. Adams' subject
for his speech was the "Importance and Necessity of Public
Faith to the Well-being of a Government." It was a topic
of timely importance, for in 1787 the little confederation of
states on the American shores was only four years removed
from British occupation. Already the price of liberty had
proved high, and some citizens and state governments found
themselves in doubt as to whether it was worth paying so
much for national unity.

John Quincy Adams had achieved his Harvard education
and it was forever a deep satisfaction to him. Even as a youth,
his preoccupation with education and political affairs was
notable. Yet it was not an unusual preoccupation, particularly when placed against John Quincy Adams' belief from
childhood that he was destined to rise high in the service
of his nation.

Adams had come home at 18, a pleasant oval-faced youth
who could discourse quite learnedly in European circles on
the classics. If, today, that would appear to be an accomplish-
ment of little usefulness outside scholastic circles, that was
not the case in the eighteenth century. Diplomats then
found at least one area in which they could be unfailingly
pleasant to one another and to which they could turn in
complete accord: the classics. Frenchman, Englishman,
Prussian, Italian, and even Russian could talk quietly, without heat, of the accomplishments of Claudius Ptolemaeus,
the great astronomer, or of Grotius, or Marcus Aurelius. If
it seemed unrealistic to carry on extended dinner conversations, week in and week out, about people and events long
dead, at least such formality provided an atmosphere in

which negotiation on current issues could prosper. Young
John Quincy Adams had grasped this subtlety and had con-
centrated thereafter on preparing himself for a life in public
service. His anxiety, lest he become a citizen of two nations
and thus of none, stemmed from contact with Europeans
and Americans who had done just that—including a loose-
limbed young grandson of Benjamin Franklin who was
equally looseheaded. This bearer of the Franklin name
wasted his days in Paris in pleasure, carried a cat outdoors
on a ribbon to walk in the ultimate of Parisian fashion, and
did not give a hang whether he ever came home or not. It
was apparent to John Quincy Adams that this particular acquaintance would never amount to anything, and the hor-
rible example spurred him on to greater efforts of his own.

One of John Quincy Adams' personality problems, even
as a youth, was an almost complete lack of humor. He was
a harsh young man, born in a harsh time. He judged himself
harshly and worried incessantly about his failures. He also
judged others harshly, and if this was only in keeping with
his spirit, his contemporaries did not always find it easy to
accept his sharp criticisms and haughty manners.

Samuel Flagg Bemis, the distinguished biographer of this
man, put it succinctly when he said that "It cannot be said
that John Quincy Adams made life at Harvard more color-
ful." He came home from Europe wearing a tricorn hat,
waistcoat, silver buckles on his shoes, and the breeches and
tailcoat that were in fashion there. He entered Harvard and
adopted Harvard ways, but he was known for his stand-
offishness as much as for his brilliance. One time, when
Harvard students went across the river to celebrate the
building of a new bridge at a barbecue on Bunker hill,
Adams stayed home, in an almost deserted college, because
he thought that the place where men fell and died in defense
of Liberty should not be profaned by gaiety.

He was a strange youth, all the more strange when his

attitudes were placed against his background and his years in Paris, the gayest and most abandoned of all European capitals. But Adams was ever to be a strict moralist, and it might have been that the very abandon of the Paris of the late eighteenth century drove him to the other extreme.

At any rate, in college Adams drank cider and smoked and talked endlessly with his peers, but only on serious subjects. He was heeding in every way an injunction from his father to value morals above all else in life.

The years at Harvard leavened John Quincy Adams, or brought him to a point of leavening. Afterwards, there was no hesitation as to his next course. He must prepare to earn a living, and since he had neither background nor inclination to follow medicine, farming, banking, or another respectable occupation, John Quincy Adams began the study of law in the office of Theophilus Parsons at Newburyport in his home state.

Despite his European upbringing Adams was Americanized—almost. The light headiness of cider gave way before the bite of strong drink in the evenings. He went out, in the company of other young men to serenade young ladies of the towns and villages underneath their windows, and Adams sometimes brought his flute along to guide faltering voices.

The year 1788 was an important one for John Quincy Adams. His family came home from Europe that year, relieving the young man of the anxieties of loneliness. He became twenty-one, achieving an independence that meant even more in the eighteenth century than it was to mean later, for in that period in America, young men and women were truly subject to the parental rule until they became mature in the eyes of the law. But most important, for Adams' own future, was the negative course of a love affair during this year.

John Quincy Adams, the young law student, fell in love with Mary Frazier, daughter of a respected citizen of Newburyport. For a time Adams and the eighteen-year-old girl talked of marriage. Both were in love. They went dancing together at Sawyer's Tavern, where young men and women gathered. They went sleighing and on hay rides, and she was serenaded more than once.

In the end, duty conquered love. Young Adams and young Miss Frazier decided that he was too poor for them to marry, that his prospects for the future were too uncertain. They parted then, with mutual promises that neither would disgrace the other by marrying someone less worthy. It was a tragic end to love, and had it not occurred, the course of John Quincy Adams' life might have been changed. But then, sacrifice of personal desire for duty was in the Adams family tradition, the frosty, conscience-driven tradition of New England, which later drove the Adamses, father and son, away from such old friends as Thomas Jefferson.

The father, John Adams, was elected Vice-President of the United States in 1788, when George Washington was elected President. In a sense, this was a compromise election between North and South, whose traditions were so different. When Washington, the Virginian, was accompanied in office by Adams, the Massachusetts man, extremists in all the colonies were fairly well-satisfied.

It was not long after the first presidential election that political differences began to appear in the states. Washington, in a sense, was beyond politics and beyond criticism. The differences that affected the life of John Quincy Adams concerned his father and the old family friend Thomas Jefferson.

In a preface to Tom Paine's *Rights of Man,* Thomas Jefferson had indicated that John Adams was straying from the revolutionary path, the path which had brought America

freedom and opportunity. John Quincy Adams took this
occasion to defend his father and also to engage in political
controversy. Under the pseudonym Publicola he wrote a
series of articles which were published in the *Columbian
Centinel* in Boston. They criticized Paine's position that
Englishmen ought to throw off the yoke of royalty and form
their own republic with a written constitution. Young
Adams took a more conservative view, a view more akin to
that of his father, who admired aristocrats and believed in
a system of class privilege. This was the beginning of an important division in American politics which was to be
brought to a climax some forty years later when Adams the
son was President.

few Americans in those days. Washington's appointment was accepted by the United States Senate without dissent, and at the age of twenty-seven, John Quincy Adams was launched in a public career in his own right.

The adult Adams had changed considerably from the slender youth who returned so well-dressed from France in 1785. He was under normal height and had begun to grow stocky. He had also begun to grow careless in dress, in spite of his mother's admonitions. He was also already a little impatient with the world, because he had not yet accomplished anything he wished, nor had he become rich enough to support himself without salary or assistance from any outside source.

On news of the appointment, which he received from his pleased father, John Quincy Adams journeyed to Philadelphia where he was asked to dinner by President Washington and by other notables. He did not go to Philadelphia for social reasons, however, but to pry into the files of the Department of State and to learn what he could of American-Dutch affairs, and also of the general affairs of America abroad.

Accompanied by his brother, Thomas Boylston Adams, the young diplomat sailed for England on September 15, 1794, and a month and a half later arrived at the Hague. He had scarcely settled into lodgings when the Low Countries were shaken by revolution. William V, the Stadtholder of Holland, had sided with the English in their war against France, although the sympathy of the Dutch people was with the French Republicans. France had dispatched a force to the Low Countries. This expeditionary army began winning victories. Within a few weeks the Stadtholder resigned his post, and fled to England. The States-General immediately voted to establish a republic.

Most diplomats left the country, dismayed and confused,

when this action came in mid-January, 1795. John Quincy Adams stood his ground. The people who were involved in this new republic, for the most part, were men who represented the parties which had forced the recognition of America in the days when Adams' father was minister to Holland. Consequently, in behalf of the American government, Adams recognized the new republic without delay.

Before the end of the month, French troops had entered the Hague, and the French exploitation of the Low Countries had begun. Adams lost no time in paying a call on the French representatives in the Hague. Here his background served him well, for when the French asked politely if he knew France, he could answer that he had grown up there in some part, and that he had studied there extensively. The French ministers were impressed. Further, Adams' background as secretary to his father and his great knowledge of diplomatic forms allowed him to pay and receive compliments from these envoys without being in the slightest confused or deluded by them.

France was more than mildly annoyed at the American attitude towards the European wars. The French were particularly vexed by a trade treaty which had just been signed by John Jay and English representatives. But Adams impressed them well, and managed, by a show of neutrality to men he secretly detested, to maintain the strength of his position in this listening-post diplomatic job in Europe.

The French government in Paris began to intrigue against the American government, and to arouse some Americans to the French cause. The motive? Always the same, hatred of England, an emotion it was not too difficult to arouse in the breasts of some Americans just a quarter century after the Revolution.

President George Washington did not want to run for reelection in 1796, but he did want to make sure that the

United States remained aloof from the turmoils and intrigues of a Europe that was divided into two armed camps. He was aided in this aim by the letters sent home to the State Department by John Quincy Adams. Many of these, and the private letters of Adams to his father, were shown to Washington. Apparently they had some effect on Washington's preparation, with Alexander Hamilton, of the Farewell Address, in which the first President warned against entanglement with foreign governments.

In the summer of 1795, John Quincy Adams was ordered to turn his Dutch post over to a charge d'affaires, temporarily. Timothy Pickering, the new American Secretary of State, wanted him to go to London to straighten out some twisted problems that had arisen in the treaty of commerce between England and the United States.

Adams sailed for London. There he encountered George Hammond, Undersecretary of Foreign Affairs, who tried to bait him into taking sides on national issues. He held a tiresome conversation with that tiresome monarch, George III, whose political blindness had brought about the rebellion of the American nation. As a young American in a delicate position, Adams was shunted about by the British foreign office until he was much upset. He was extremely pleased when the American minister to Britain returned to again take over the duties of representing the United States at the British court.

During this period, Adams yielded to a request from his family that he begin looking for a wife, although not quite in the manner they had expected.

He began courting Louisa Catherine Johnson, daughter of the American consul, Joshua Johnson, who was the brother of the one-time governor of Maryland. Johnson had gone to England before the revolution to represent a firm in Annapolis, and he had remained in Europe. During the revolution he had moved to France, which stamped him as a patriot, but he had also married an English wife which brought some criticism.

In Joshua Johnson's case the criticism did not matter. He was consul in England, and an English wife made it easier, not harder, to do business with the English. But the children of that union were not regarded in America as full Americans, and when John Quincy Adams announced to his mother that he was planning to marry the Johnson girl, Abigail Adams was not at all pleased, and old John Adams was worried lest his marriage affect his son's career badly.

Abigail Adams suggested that perhaps John still had some obligation to his young sweetheart, Mary Frazier. It was too bad she had not taken that attitude years before, when John Quincy's ardor was aflame. Distance and the years had led the young man and the girl he once loved far apart. Now, in 1796, he was ready for marriage, and he found in this twenty-one-year-old Louisa Johnson what he wanted. It was not a love match. He indicated that repeatedly in his diary. But neither was the marriage one of convenience in the normal sense. John Quincy was ready to settle down, Louisa was equally ready—even a bit past her prime as young English gentlewomen were inclined to view such affairs. In 1797 they were married in England, as he came through that land once more on his way to a new post as minister to Lisbon.

In Boston, the news of this marriage brought immediate political repercussions. The nation had split now, politically, into Federalist and Republican political factions. The Republican *Independent Chronicle* of Boston noted that young Adams' "negotiations" had ended in a marriage treaty with a young Englishwoman. It was fortunate for the nation, said the newspaper, that Adams had not negotiated any other treaty in behalf of America.

The Federalist *Columbian Centinel* responded to that attack in defense of Adams. The young lady was an American (said the newspaper, disregarding her English mother). Further, young Adams was a worthy representative of the United States abroad.

But Abigail Adams was right in one sense. She had worried lest this marriage be a burden to her son, and politically, it was to become a burden in later years. Even when Adams was President of the United States, political opponents were to refer tellingly to his "English wife."

Once Adams and Louisa Johnson were married, they prepared to set off by ship for Portugal. President Washington promoted him from Minister Resident to Minister Plenipotentiary. This meant more than acquiring a resounding title—it doubled Adams' salary, from $4500 to $9000 a year and made it possible for the young diplomat to save money.

Probably Washington's promotion was made to save John Adams embarrassment, for when Washington had declined to run for a third term, John Adams, Vice-President, in a close contest with Thomas Jefferson, was elected to succeed him.

In those days the electoral college functioned differently. The American system, after all, was just a few years old. Political parties, as such, had not yet appeared, although out of the factionalism that arose in reference to the French revolution came political differences that were important enough to split the revolutionaries.

One hundred and thirty-eight electors, chosen by the state legislatures, voted in the election of 1796. Of these, 71 voted for John Adams and 68 for Thomas Jefferson. This meant that Adams was to be President—an Adams who held the Hamiltonian or restricted-democracy view of government. He believed, like his son, that the English system of political freedom was essentially sound. He saw nothing

wrong with the creation of an aristocracy and he abhorred
the idea of placing power directly in the hands of the people.
To be Vice-president now was Thomas Jefferson, that old
friend of Adams who had diverged in his views. For actually
it could be said that Adams had remained steadfast, cling-
ing to a system he had known all his life, although he agreed
from the beginning with Jefferson and others on the intoler-
ability of English rule. Jefferson had become enthusiastic
about the French revolution and had remanied so through
all that revolution's excesses. Under the undeveloped
American political system, then, if Adams were to die in
office, his political opponent and opposite would become
President of the United States. It was fortunate that the
American people had ceased, by this time, to be totally
violent in nature.

The new President, in consultation with Washington,
again promoted his son, and John Quincy Adams, ready to
sail for Lisbon, was flabbergasted to learn that he was not
to go to Lisbon at all, but to establish a new American diplomatic post in Prussia. At first, although the job was more
important, Adams was upset. He had spent $2500 to rent
a house in Lisbon. He had made all his plans. But luckily,
he soon adjusted to the idea, and was fortunate enough to
have three full months of honeymoon in England with his
new bride before Congress settled the details of the new
appointment.

In America, there was some criticism of President Adams
for appointing his son to a high post. There was more criticism in Congress of the administration's action in extend-
ing the American diplomatic service by adding another embassy. The objection was not solely a monetary one. Nearly
all Americans of any influence were basically very wary of
Europe and European affairs. And why should they not be?
After all, this was the period in which the struggle for

supremacy between France and England reached its peak. A French general named Napoleon Bonaparte was storming through Italy. All Europe seemed a bloody cockpit in which the birds lashed at everything that moved. Americans wanted no part of European affairs. This one principle dominated all else.

In October, 1797, Adams and his bride set out for Berlin. They traveled quickly enough to Hamburg by ship. But from Hamburg to Berlin the route was overland, and progress was slow. A friend told Adams that he could not expect to travel over the German roads at a speed of more than two hours to every mile, so atrocious were the roads! Their coach broke down. They were forced to stay in a German inn and sleep between two feather beds, which Adams disliked intensely. They traveled through sleet and rain and what seemed to be an endless sea of mud but finally in November they reached Berlin.

In Berlin, at first Adams' duties seemed largely limited to card parties, balls, and reviews of the troops. If he failed to attend any official or semi-official function, his absence was noted, and became subject for comment. But Adams was far more interested in the productive aspects of his mission. He attempted to purchase arms, and he negotiated a trade treaty with the Prussian government.

He was successful in his negotiations and here, once again, proved himself an able diplomat. Afterward, when he had established himself in Berlin, he found time to travel about Germany, perfecting his command of the language and learning much about the people and politics. His wife was not particularly happy in Berlin, largely because the climate disagreed with her. They traveled for a number of weeks in Silesia, an area not usually visited by Americans.

Adams' father, President of the United States, was unfortunate enough to arouse considerable animosity within the ranks of his own Federalist party, and in the election of 1800 he was unseated by Thomas Jefferson. John Quincy Adams, generally speaking, shared the views of his father on foreign affairs, views that included a deep distrust of the direction in which the French revolutionary government was moving. Young Adams believed that the French were moving towards absolute control of the nation by one person, and that when this occurred, France would become a serious threat to the peace of the world because she would seek to enlarge her empire—as she was already doing even when Adams went on his first diplomatic mission to Holland.

Despite the divergence of his views from those of Jefferson, John Quincy Adams was so well respected on his own merits that he might well have continued in the foreign service indefinitely. In the beginning, he had determined that he would devote only three years to service abroad. He had come to like the work, however, and as Minister Plenipotentiary he was well enough paid that he need not worry about money. Should he remain in Europe?

The question was quickly answered, not by any action or indication on the part of Thomas Jefferson, but by President John Adams. He ordered his son to come home.

Perhaps the President feared that his son's continuation in the diplomatic service under Jefferson would be an embarrassment to the family. Perhaps, in his arbitrary fashion, old John Adams simply decided that it was time for the young man to come home and settle down. He was capable of making such a decision without giving any thought to his son's wishes.

At any rate, the decision was made, and John Quincy Adams was ordered to return to the United States. He traveled to Potsdam where he was received at the palace by both the King and Queen of Prussia, then said his farewells to

Berlin and boarded the ship *America* at Hamburg, on July 8, 1801. In September the ship landed at Philadelphia, and John Quincy Adams and his wife parted for a while—he to go to Quincy to visit his mother and father, and she to go to Maryland, to visit her parents who had returned to the United States to live.

Adams had been away from America for seven years. It seemed now that one career was behind him, and another was about to begin—and that the new career would not be in government but in practice of the law.

☆ ☆ ☆

CHAPTER 3

Politician and Professor

IN SEVEN years abroad, John Quincy Adams had been able to save money on his salary as minister, quite unlike the ministers and ambassadors of later years, who had to dig deep into their pockets to support their activities as representatives of the United States.

Adams had saved so much that when he returned to America he had assets of $43,000, including two houses in Boston and more than $10,000 in U.S. securities. It was a respectable fortune, not large, but enough to give Adams time to establish himself in the practice of law.

He returned to the law soberly, if not with any great enthusiasm. As a diplomat he had grown rusty, so he began once again to study his lawbooks and to take great pains to bring himself up to date on the law. In those formative years of the Republic, great changes were taking place in the American attitude toward the common law. While the original 13 colonies had at first banded together in loose federation, they were discovering that defense, the national economy, physical improvements, and that debatable subject—the national welfare—demanded relinquishment of ever more local power to the federal government.

Not all Americans were agreed on this policy. In fact, the question of centralism vs. local power was as important as the differences in foreign policy which led to establishment of a party system. In Washington's day the Americans were all revolutionaries together. But less than two years of John Adams' term had gone by when serious differences appeared. Old John Adams cared nothing for politics. If people wanted to call him a Federalist, he would prefer to call himself a Nationalist. His son shared that view. On his return to the United States, having observed what had occurred during his absence, John Quincy Adams wrote in his journal that he felt a strong temptation to plunge into the political controversies of the day.

"But I hope to preserve myself from it," he also wrote, "by the considerations which have led me to the resolution of renouncing. A politician in this country must be the man of a party. I would fain be the man of my whole country."

And just what had happened in America in the seven years in which John Quincy Adams had been serving his nation overseas?

Alexander Hamilton, the real leader of the Federalists, had led that group toward a policy of strong central control of the economy and the governing power. It might be said that neither George Washington nor John Adams were truly Federalists, at least neither was a "party man", but the same could not be said of Hamilton, who was intensely partisan in his approach to public affairs.

Hamilton had been responsible for the building of a strong, central Treasury Department when he was Washington's Secretary of the Treasury. He had forced the establishment of a central banking system, over the complaints of others who said the federal government was taking too much power away from the states. He had brought about the first national tax—the excise tax on liquor—and had caused a display of federal power in tax collection when Federal troops were used to put down the Whiskey Rebellion in Pennsylvania. He had initiated the first national tariff—the first tax on imported goods.

The financial system invented by Hamilton did what he wanted it to do. It brought in enough money to support the activities of the federal government without grants from the state governments. The financial plan was successful then, and it seemed eminently sensible to the important business-men of the day. They put themselves behind Hamilton, and the Federalist party became a party allied with business interests.

The Federalists distrusted the French revolutionaries who had so little regard for property rights, and they leaned heavily toward the British system. John Adams and his son were Federalists in this respect. But Hamilton and Adams fell out, and on the eve of the Presidential election of 1800, Hamilton circulated a letter strongly critical of Adams' presidential policies.

The Republican party had taken form by this time. Its leader was Jefferson. It gained great national strength in the struggle over the Alien and Sedition Laws of 1798. These laws provided for serious penalty in case of disloyal criticism of the government and disloyal acts. But as it was to happen again and again in American history, so it happened then: who was to determine the degree of loyalty and disloyalty? And how much right did the federal government have to curb the criticisms of its citizens, or their political beliefs and actions?

Thomas Jefferson and James Madison, Republicans, took the position that John Adams, Federalist, was assuming far too much power for the federal government during his Presidency. This question, plus Jefferson's personal popularity and the issue of Adams' foreign leanings, decided the election in 1800. John Adams, a bitter man, retired to Massachusetts where the Federalists still maintained their power. John Quincy Adams came home, not at all certain that he wanted anything to do with party politics, and so personally antagonistic to Alexander Hamilton that he could never be a whole-hearted Federalist.

During the winter of 1801-1802, John Quincy Adams studied and worked at the law. He was appointed a commissioner of bankruptcies by a federal judge in the district. But within a few months Congress changed the law, providing for the appointment of permanent commissioners by the President. Jefferson did not appoint Adams—a sore point with the Adams family ever after.

In the spring of 1802, or rather early in April, just before spring came, John Quincy Adams was selected by the Federalist party as nominee for the office of state senator. He was still serving as a commissioner of bankruptcy at that time, and the opposition newspapers did not hesitate to note that Adams and another candidate for the Senate both held these jobs. How could they accept two offices?

The other candidate, William Tudor, was upset. He was already a state senator, and he feared that the adverse publicity would cost him his seat. He came to Adams' office on April 1, agitated, and said the two of them ought to prepare a paragraph for the *Centinel,* refuting the opposition claim.

Adams was much calmer and he knew exactly why. Being a senator, Tudor would be upset if he were defeated. But since Adams held no such office, he would not feel deprived if he failed to attain it. Besides, Adams confided to his diary, election would interfere with a lot of things he wanted to do.

On April 5 the Federalist ticket was elected, and both Tudor and John Quincy Adams were to be state senators.

In the state Senate, Adams took his duties as seriously as he always took any public duty. He gave full consideration to every measure, examining it according to his views on public policy and constitutionality. When a bill came up to extend the charter of the Union Bank for ten years, Adams

took no part in the debate, because he was a stockholder of
that bank.

He tried, unsuccessfully, to secure proportional representation for the Republican minority on the Governor's
Council. Members of the Federalist party did not care for
his concern for the political enemy. He fought other measures supported by the party leaders because he did not believe in them. Within a few months he had shown himself
to be an extremely independent lawmaker and had aroused
the intense dislike of the more conservative elements in the
Federalist movement. Some called him "unmanageable,"
for he was not inclined to participate in the political com-
promises that other legislators found necessary to insure
success for their bills.

Still, the name of Adams carried great weight in Massachusetts politics, and John Quincy Adams could not be ignored. He decided to seek election to the House of Representatives as Federalist candidate from the Boston district,
and he secured the nomination.

But nomination and election are two different matters.
It rained on election day. Rain, it seems, has always been
the curse of the conservatives or farm parties, for when it
rains on election day the farmers find it difficult to get to the
polls. At least that was what the Federalist politicians said
the next day. John Quincy Adams had lost the election by
59 votes only, but he had lost it as surely as if the other man
had carried Massachusetts by a landslide. Adams carried
Boston by 66 votes, but out in the country where the roads
were mud and slime in the rain, his opponent had more
than made up the difference.

Adams took occasion, privately, to blame the defeat on
the whole idea of Federalism, or political groupings. "This
is one of a thousand proofs how large a portion of Federal-

ism is a mere fair-weather principle, too weak to overcome a shower of rain". That was how he put it in his diary.

He said he was pleased with the outcome, and felt he had been relieved of a heavy burden. But this was more sour grapes than truth, obviously, for a few months later, when a vacancy occurred in the United States Senate seat from Massachusetts, Adams was an eager candidate.

Timothy Pickering seemed the logical candidate for the post. He had been Secretary of State. He was the choice of the *Essex Junto*—a strong-willed, ultra-partisan group of Federalists who wished to control the party, and were willing to form temporary liaisons with Republicans, or any others, in their efforts to do so.

But many Massachusetts Federalists disliked the *Essex Junto* as much as they disliked Republicans, and a group of these men put up John Quincy Adams' name for the Senate post.

Adams hated politicking, but it was politicking that got him the Senate post.

In those days, the House of Representatives of Massachusetts chose the men who would go to the U.S. Senate to represent the state. Some twenty members of the House met privately on the night before the decision was to be made, and considered the seven candidates for the post. Since the Federalists controlled the House, they could elect a man if they could agree on one, but not all could stomach Mr. Pickering, who had become an enemy of John Adams during the last years of his administration. At the caucus, the twenty men decided that they would vote for Pickering on two ballots but that if he was not elected then, they would swing over to John Quincy Adams in a body.

The next day, on the first ballot Pickering received 67 votes and Adams received ten. But Pickering could not be elected, that much was sure. On that ballot, Tompson J. Skinner, a political opponent, received 71 votes, the almost solid vote of the opposition.

On the second ballot Pickering picked up thirteen votes, but still not enough to win. On the third ballot, however, the switch to Adams was only partial, and not until a fourth ballot was taken did it become general. Adams, showing the family trait of irascibility, was more annoyed at the politicking than pleased at the results of his election. He was a difficult man to satisfy.

But in those days, as always, it took such men to keep government from becoming a sinkhole of special interests. Adams was given an illustration of this tendency on the very next day after his election to the U.S. Senate. He was still a state senator, and as such was serving on a committee of five men entrusted with a measure that involved the establishment of a new bank in Boston. Two members of the committee were enthusiastic about the prospects. Two members were vigorously opposed. Adams was to be the deciding voter.

Boston's businessmen wanted a new bank, and apparently one was needed. But to encourage legislative support for the charter, it was rumored, the men who planned for the new bank had set aside a number of shares which were to be gifts to the legislators who voted for the bank. Adams was outraged and worried, lest the reputation of the legislature be tarnished. He demanded that the names of the men who were subscribing to the fund for the bank be made public, or at least that the legislature know the names. The promoters objected strenuously to this publicity.

Eventually the bank bill was passed by both houses, but by this time several more important personal matters occupied Adams's attention.

As a state legislator and lawyer he was not growing wealthy, but he seemed to be holding his own financially, and he lived happily enough with his growing family in a well-furnished house he had bought at 39 Hanover street in Boston. His father, who had moved to Quincy now, seemed well-enough off, following a series of apparently successful investments, and rental of the farming properties around Braintree.

In the spring of 1803, when he was selected for the U.S. Senate, the future looked bright to John Quincy Adams once again. His wife was about to have a child, their second son. He occupied himself with scholarship in the evenings, visited friends, and threw himself into his legislative work with his usual zeal.

Then, a famous banking house to which he had assigned some bills, closed its doors after the money had been collected but before it had been paid out to the Adams family. It was all the more embarrassing because the money belonged to old John Adams who had asked his son to handle the collection for him.

The failure was serious enough that John Quincy Adams sold his Boston real estate, including the house in which he lived, to cover the losses. In an atmosphere of considerable gloom, then, Adams moved his family to Washington in the autumn of 1803 to take up his duties as United States Senator.

Washington was a miserable little town in those days. It had but one theater, and there the performances were sporadic and often anathema to lovers of the theater. It was totally an artificial city, created for the sole purpose of government. It consisted of a handful of badly designed government buildings, frame boarding-houses, a few restaurants and taverns of indifferent quality, and a milling group

of legislators, government employees and favor-seekers
who tramped through the muddy or dusty streets and
cursed the muggy climate.

Senator and Mrs. John Quincy Adams, delayed by a number of personal crises in Boston and Quincy, came to Washington when the Senate was already in session. They moved
into the home of one of Louisa's sisters, to board with the
family. So that he might have a "home," he bought from his
father the old Penn's Hill Farm where he had been born,
and during the recesses of Congress, the Adams family returned to Massachusetts for rest and visits to the home of
the former President of the United States.

In Washington, this Adams was a frequent guest at the
White House. Despite the differences that had grown between the Adams family and Jefferson, John Quincy Adams
could not help but remember that Jefferson was an old
friend who had taken him for long walks through the Bois
de Boulogne in Paris, and who had written letters of recom-
mendation for the boy when he returned to the United
States for study.

They were brought closer together, too, by a changing
climate of opinion. Jefferson had moderated his views on
the French Republic considerably since the accession to
power of Napoleon. It was apparent in 1803 that Napoleon
was bent on conquering all of Europe. Not all Americans
knew that Napoleon wanted to conquer the entire world,
but many had begun to suspect it.

In pursuit of just such hopes, Napoleon had gained control from Spain of the lands of Louisiana and the Floridas.
He had done so secretly. In 1800 his ambassador in Madrid
had signed the secret treaty of San Ildefonso which gave
Louisiana to France. Thereupon, Napoleon had set out to
establish a foothold on the North American continent. He
sent an army to the Caribbean, ostensibly to quell the Hai-

tian revolt of Toussaint L'Ouverture. But that army was supposed to put L'Ouverture down in a few days, and then proceed to Louisiana territory to dig in.

Napoleon's plans for the western world were tabled when he went to war with England, and when malaria and yellow fever decimated the French army in the new world. The war with England brought him need for money, too, and he negotiated the sale of the Louisiana territory to the United States for 60,000,000 francs ($11,250,000) plus another 20,000,000 francs which the United States would pay to U.S. citizens for debts owed by the French government.

So, for about $15,000,000 the youthful United States of America doubled its territory. The land included 828,000 square miles which lay between the Mississippi river and the Rocky Mountains. How far south did it extend? To the Gulf of Mexico, that much was certain, but that was all that was certain. The remainder—Texas, for example—would be determined in later years. And the purchase made no specific mention of the Florida territory, which also was to create problems in the future.

It was no simple matter for President Jefferson to negotiate the purchase of this territory. Nowhere in the Constitution had it been stated that the executive (or anyone else) had the specific right to buy lands. Jefferson took the view that this was very much the business of the executive and of the government. The Federalists in Congress took the position that this was not the business of the executive, in particular.

Senator Adams had not arrived in Washington in time to vote on the treaty by which the United States annexed Louisiana. That fact alone prevented him from being subjected to criticism by his party from the very beginning of his term of office, for all the Federalists in the Senate voted against the treaty. Luckily for the future of the nation,

there were only seven Federalists in the Senate at that time,
as compared to 24 Republicans, who voted for the measure.

But Senator Adams did not let much time elapse before
showing where his sympathies lay. He voted for a bill that
created bonds to pay the purchase price. He wrote in favor
of the measure but he parted company with Jefferson on
the method of governing the new territory, on the principle
of no taxation without representation. He supported Federalist positions in some other respects, but it was apparent
before long that any relationship between John Quincy
Adams and the Federalists was simply coincidental. He
went so far as to attend a celebration dinner in honor of the
Louisiana Purchase—one held by the hated Republicans.

At this particular time, the leading Federalists of Massachusetts had formed themselves into a truly revolutionary
pressure group. The *Essex Junto* had secession in its mind,
and it was, or appeared to be, gaining the power to carry out
the plans of its leaders.

Shortly after John Quincy Adams had been selected to
serve the full six year term as Senator from Massachusetts,
Timothy Pickering, his opponent for the job, had been
chosen to fill a shorter term. Pickering was the leader of the
Essex Junto, and from this new position in Washington he
was able to exercise a considerable strength of leverage.

The plan of the *Essex Junto* was to establish a Northern
Confederacy. The group had been named in 1781 by John
Hancock, who called attention to this crowd from Essex
County, Massachusetts, who were apt to become violent if
the French Revolution was mentioned favorably. Hatred
of the French revolution led to hatred of the principles of
popular democracy in all they stood for. By the turn of the
century, the *Essex Junto* represented an absolute extreme
of opinion which in the twentieth century would have been
called the extreme right wing.

The *Junto* hoped to create a new nation composed of the five New England states, New York, and New Jersey. Central to the plan, however, was the election of Aaron Burr as governor of New York. Burr ran for governor in 1804. Alexander Hamilton opposed Burr's ambitions and frustrated them. That summer Hamilton and Burr dueled, Hamilton was mortally wounded, and on his death Burr went into hiding. *The Essex Junto* continued its secret planning, but the impetus was lost. And while Burr and others in this period of political realignment were to continue to try to undermine the federal government in Washington, they were not to succeed.

As far as John Quincy Adams was concerned, there was no proof of the evil plans of the *Essex Junto* conspirators. He knew of the existence of the conspiracy, but the Essex men knew Adams well enough to know that he would never participate in such a scheme. They spent their efforts attempting to promote national disunity with as much enthusiasm as Adams spent in the cause of national unity. The result was that Adams found himself bending ever more toward the positions of the Republicans in Congress. This independence pleased no one. The Republicans were grateful for Adams' support on specific issues, but he was not a Republican, and they did not return the favors.

The Federalists, split and dying as the party was, soon broke with Adams. He was "like a kite without a tail" sneered Boston Banker Stephen Higginson. He was dangerous and uncontrollable, said Senator Pickering, who at fifty-nine was junior Senator from Massachusetts while the stocky Adams at thirty-six was senior Senator.

John Quincy Adams, privately, was not the self-contained and confident man that Senator Adams appeared to be. He spent many long evenings in the quiet of his study or his bedroom deep in self-examination. He spoke and wrote then, of the "errors, impudences and follies" he had committed. He worried about pride and self-conceit, and presumption which he felt stained his character. He was not kindly to other men, in thought or deed, but neither was he kindly to himself. He was, even at thirty-six, a tortured soul, dedicated to, but miserably sensitive to public and private criticism.

By the beginning of 1804, Adams was also quite aware of the political folly of his attitude towards political parties, and his refusal to follow a party line in public affairs. He knew that he ran the danger of being unseated. Yet he had made his choice—to vote according to conscience—and he was determined to stick with that choice.

These were important days, and Senator John Quincy Adams was an important man. He might be found in the office or on the Senate floor or at home. He might be dining with the Vice-President, or calling on Mr. Jefferson at home and listening to some of Jefferson's wild parlor stories, such as one in which he claimed to have learned Spanish in nineteen days at sea with a copy of Don Quixote. Or were they parlor stories? Jefferson was a brilliant scholar and quite capable of such a feat. Adams was never quite sure how much Jefferson was spoofing.

The life of a United States Senator in those years was more tranquil than it was later to become. In 1805 Senator Adams spent but five months in Washington. He was in the nation's capital in January, February, and March, and again in November and December, at which times the Senate was in session. The rest of the year was spent traveling to and from Quincy and staying with his father and mother.

At Quincy he spent some time working on the farm, but soon gave it up as a waste of time he would rather use for other purposes. He retreated again to his studies of the classics. He spent no time at all in political fence-mending, although he noted at the end of the year that his political prospects were sadly declining.

Senator Adams might be disliked by many of his colleagues for his blunt manner of pursuing an object or a point. He might be enemy to most of the Federalists who lingered on in the Senate, and an object of mild suspicion to all the Republicans, but he was respected. He became one of the hardest-working Senators in that body, and his services were demanded for one special committee after another.

In the summer of 1805, Adams was appointed professor of Rhetoric and Oratory at Harvard, a job he accepted with some gladness, although he had to confine his teaching, in the beginning, to the summer period when Congress would not be in session. He did not expect to be so very long in the Senate, however. His term was due to expire in 1809, and he fully expected to be defeated if he ran again for the office. On hearing of his appointment, he planned a seven year program of scholarship for himself in this field. And there is every indication that he would have been pleased to have settled down in Boston to a life of teaching and study of his own.

The following year Adams bought another house in Boston and gave indications that he was preparing to settle down once the Senatorial term ended.

But the end of his Senate career came even earlier than John Quincy Adams had expected, in a blowup in Massachusetts politics over a grave issue of foreign relations.

Years before, when Adams was serving abroad, he had discussed the question of impressment of seamen from American ships by British naval vessels. No adequate solution to the problem had ever been found—and in truth, the Eng-

lish had some justification, for a great number of English
sailors deserted under the harsh discipline of His Majesty's
Navy and found softer berths on American ships.

Still, the English continued the arrogant practice of
stopping vessels on the high seas and removing men, deserters or not, as they chose. The British captain alone made
the decision which might mean life or death for the men
involved, and certainly did mean humiliation and manning
problems for the American ships from which crewmen were
taken. American captains quivered with rage at these board-
ings. American shipowners raged even more at the British
blockade and cargo seizures. The United States, after all,
was a neutral in the wars between England and the continental nations. But Britain ruled the seas and countenanced
no neutrality. She seized ships and cargoes bound for her
enemies, and some which her seamen only claimed were so
bound.

The disputes had been going on for more than a decade,
and the Americans had become wily blockade runners, who
often carried two sets of papers—one set to show British
boarders and the other for the French. The Americans were
torn between their annoyance with British high-handed-
ness, their distaste for French methods, and fear of Napoleon's ambition.

It was annoying enough to have British men of war stop
American merchant vessels. On June 22, 1807, a British
captain in American waters took another action that turned
out to be fatal to relations between the two nations. This
officer, commander of *HMS Leopard,* a frigate, stopped the
USS Chesapeake, an American frigate. The commander ordered the American vessel to heave to, and permit search
for four men whom the British claimed were deserters. The
American captain refused to permit search, so *Leopard*
opened fire without notice, killing three men and wounding

eighteen, and forcing the unprepared *Chesapeake* to surrender. Thereupon, the British captain took off four men. One, a real deserter, they hanged. The other three were impressed into the British navy forcibly, as thousands of other Americans had been in years past, and thousands more would be, until the end of the War of 1812.

When news of this indignity against the American flag was made known in Boston, John Quincy Adams was in the city, teaching at Harvard for the summer. Immediately, he called on Federalist leaders to hold a mass indignation meeting.

The call caught the Federalists in a difficult position. They had long espoused the cause of more friendly relations with Great Britain. The Republicans of the area had no such worries. They held a mass meeting, which Adams attended and helped draw up resolutions of protest in addition, to the embarrassment of the Federalists.

President Jefferson called Congress into session a month and a half earlier than usual that year, because feeling across the nation was running high in the wake of the *Chesapeake-Leopard* affair. Congress was ready to do something, but not very much. Adams was chairman of a committee that reported out a bill forbidding British ships the use of American waters. But no call to arms was made, and in the absence of one, the British government did not take the American annoyance very seriously.

The issue hung before the nation all during the autumn of 1807. Then Jefferson heard of even harsher measures that were to be taken by the British government. He consulted with Congressional leaders of the Republican party, and decided to ask for an embargo on all American shipping. The purpose was to keep American ships out of British hands, and American goods out of the hands of both belligerent powers—England and France.

The businessmen who depended on shipping and trade were furious, and they called upon all the support they could muster from the deteriorating Federalist movement.

No Boston banker could now sneer that John Quincy Adams was a kite without a tail. Senator Adams joined the Republicans on this issue and voted for the embargo, along with 21 Republican senators. The six Federalists voted against it.

The following month, the first of the year 1808, Senator Adams attended a caucus of the Republican party to select candidates for President and Vice-President. This was outright admission that he had switched his allegiance from the Federalists.

The Republicans were loud in their praise of John Quincy Adams, but even his father believed that Adams had sealed his political fate forever. He wrote, with characteristic bossiness, that his son ought to give up all politics and return to his professorship and the law, and devote himself to the education of his children. That was tantamount to telling John Quincy that he was finished in public affairs.

The Massachusetts legislators who had put John Quincy Adams into the Senate were annoyed, as well. The legislature met in May, 1808, at a time when Boston and the Massachusetts manufacturers were beginning to feel the bite of the Jefferson embargo on trade. By a vote of 248 to 213 the legislature chose James Lloyd, Jr. as successor to Adams in the Senate. It was six months before the normal date for an election to the Senate, and obviously was intended to be a personal rebuke to Senator Adams. He took it as such and immediately resigned from the Senate. It appeared that his father was right and that John Quincy Adams' political career was at an end.

☆ ☆ ☆

CHAPTER 4

The Rising Diplomat

IN BOSTON in the summer of 1808, Professor John Quincy
Adams divided his time between teaching at Harvard college, rebuilding his slender law practice, and fending off efforts by Republican political leaders in Massachusetts to
persuade him to return to politics.

There was no question but what he wanted to return to
politics. He also told the Republicans who came to call that
he believed their cause was the proper one. But personal
considerations entered into his thinking, too. The incum-
bent member of Congress from Boston was Josiah Quincy,
an old friend of the Adams family. This was the post the
Republicans wanted Adams to seek, for in running for the
House he would be elected by the people and not by the
legislature, which was safely in control of the Federalists at
that moment.

Adams continued to support Jefferson's foreign policy
with the considerable amount of influence he retained, particularly with friends in Congress. His enemies, naturally
enough, claimed that the short-tempered professor was
currying favor and sought some post from the Republicans.
Adams did not discount the idea, but it was not in his nature
to take any position simply for personal gain. He had supported the Republicans in the Senate knowing full well that
it meant political suicide in Massachusetts at that time. He
continued along his lonely, rugged path.

How easy it would have been for John Quincy Adams, at any point before 1808, to have joined the men of privilege who made up the controlling faction of Massachusetts politics. By nature, he belonged to this group; they would have accepted him wholeheartedly. By nature, too, he was not a democrat of the Jeffersonian persuasion. He continued to believe that power and prestige belonged by right to an elite corps in the nation, and this was not strange. Nearly all the men with whom Adams associated were men of privilege and at least some wealth and education—Jefferson among them. But John Quincy Adams was far more a democrat than his father had been in his youth. The French Revolution and Jeffersonian policies had changed the original concept of the American republic even in the eyes of most of the men who had served in government in the early years. From the very moment of the signing of the Articles of Confederation, the United States government was in the process of change and growth. The change was unending.

A symptom of the change in government in America is to be found in the next overture made to John Quincy Adams. In the late winter of 1809, Adams went to Washington to argue a law case before the United States Supreme Court. He was in the capital city when President James Madison was inaugurated, and he and his mother-in-law attended the ceremony in the House of Representatives. Later they drove over to Madison's residence to pay their respects. Madison was not yet living in the White House because Jefferson had not yet moved out. The practice of immediate vacation of the White House by the outgoing President was something for the future, to come when politics brought enemies face to face. Madison was no enemy, but a Republican like Jefferson.

While Adams was in Washington, he received a note to come to see President Madison. The note was marked urgent, and Madison was urgent. He told the former Senator that he wanted to nominate him as minister to Russia. It was to be a new post. The reason for creating the post was to establish trade and diplomatic relations with the government of the Czar. And the reason for that was the conquest of Europe by Napoleon. It was apparent to the Madison Administration that America needed all the friends she could get.

John Quincy Adams accepted the post on the spot. He had to, for President Madison gave him less than half an hour to make up his mind. But Adams was doubtful if the Senate would confirm the nomination, and he was correct in his estimate.

Thomas Jefferson had proposed to establish diplomatic relations with Russia a year before and had nominated a minister. But the Senate had refused to confirm the appointment. The legislators were not at all anxious to extend the power and scope of government, particularly in the field of foreign affairs. And in this period of history, there was no question of the Administration applying excessive pressure to the legislative body. Each branch of the government tried jealously to guard its prerogatives. The Judiciary had just come through a frightening attempt by the Congress to impose its will on the judges, an attempt accompanied by efforts to impeach several judges whose decisions Congressmen did not like. And each time the Executive branch proposed creation of a new office, the proposal was given long and hard examination by the Congress, to see if it extended Executive power unduly, or if it would bring excessive additions to the cost of government.

In the case of the mission to Russia, the Senate decided once again that the idea was not a good one. Adams, disappointed as anyone who accepts an appointment must be, returned to Boston and to his professorship, which interested him, and to the law, by which he supported himself.

But the Senate of the United States changed its mind. In March, the vote had been 17 to 15 against establishment of any mission at all. On June 27, the vote was 19 to 7 to appoint John Quincy Adams minister to Russia. Of the seven senators who voted negatively, two were Republicans who still did not believe in the mission. Five were Federalists who hated John Quincy Adams as a turncoat.

What had happened to change the minds of the senators?

For one thing, the French had invaded Portugal and threatened Lisbon. If they succeeded in conquering the British forces there, they would control the entire Iberian peninsula, for they had already driven the British from Spain.

To the east, the French had put down a rebellion among the German people. The Archduke Charles of Austria called upon all the Germanic peoples to unite against Napoleon, raised an army of 170,000 men, and in April, invaded Bavaria. Napoleon was in Spain, but he hurried east, and led his troops in battle. The French drove the Archduke's forces across the Danube in a series of battles, and then took Vienna. Napoleon was halted temporarily in May, but no one believed that was the end of the action in the east, and the Senate of the United States suddenly saw the wisdom of the original Jeffersonian proposal.

In 1809, news traveled slowly from Washington. It came up to Philadelphia by coach, to New York by ship and coach, and then over the Boston Post Road to Boston. It reached John Quincy Adams seven days after the appointment was confirmed by the Senate. Adams, at that time, was attending a Fourth of July celebration.

As he did so often in his mature years, Adams stopped to take stock of himself on the eve of his mission to Russia. He was 42 years old. He was growing bald, and the lines of stern New England were etched in his bony face. He still hoped ultimately to hold himself above political parties, but by now he was well aware of the grim realities in the processes of government. He was convinced that the new administration would aim at the welfare of the Union, and he was willing to support it.

On August 5 Adams and his wife and small son Charles Francis boarded the ship *Horace* at William Gray's wharf in Charlestown, and set off for St. Petersburg. The two elder Adams boys, George Washington and John, were left behind, to continue their educations in America in the care of other members of the family. Two of Adams' Harvard students accompanied the minister, much as he had accompanied Francis Dana a quarter of a century before, but not at all for the same reasons. He had gone with Dana in 1782 because Dana needed an interpreter who could speak French. In those years few Americans were equipped to deal on equal terms with the cultured and sophisticated diplomats of Europe. But in 1809 John Quincy Adams was admirably equipped to hold his own in any company or society. He spoke French and German very well, had a smattering of other living languages, and was a master of the classics. His bright mind had been quickened by the responsibilities and challenges of life in the United States Senate, which demands the utmost of every man if he wishes to legislate and not sit on the sidelines. He had, also, a respected background as professor at one of America's finest colleges, and if American colleges were not yet highly regarded in England and elsewhere, still there was magic in the title when used in Europe.

On the *Horace's* voyage to Russia, it became quite apparent to John Quincy Adams that his services as minister could be immediately valuable to his country in one way. It was a long voyage—75 days—and they met every kind of weather. Adams had set off believing that there would be no question of warlike action against the American ship, for America was determinedly at peace with all the world, and her neutrality, she hoped, was respected.

But France and England respected no neutrality at this stage of the Napoleonic conflict. In the Baltic the *Horace* was fired upon by a British man of war and stopped and boarded. Only because Minister Adams was aboard was she allowed to proceed. Otherwise she would have been diverted from her mission.

Scarcely had the British boarding party left the ship when she was boarded by Frenchmen who were far more demanding. They warned the captain against putting in at a Danish port, but finally they allowed the ship to go in at Elsinur, and there John Quincy Adams found a fleet of American ships which Napoleon's men were holding in the harbor to prevent them from carrying supplies to or from England.

The *Horace* docked on the Neva river in St. Petersburg on October 23, a few days before ice closed the harbor of the Bay of Kronstadt. Napoleon, having defeated Austria decisively, was at the height of his power. Alexander I of Russia was technically an ally of Napoleon at this time, but Alexander was beginning to look upon Napoleon with considerable distrust. In this atmosphere Adams was able to use his persuasive powers to good ends. He interceded with Alexander, and Alexander was persuaded to release the American ships he held in virtual captivity, and to use his influence with the French to the same end. In that sense, the American mission to St. Petersburg was successful from the beginning.

Socially, the Adams family was in great demand in St. Petersburg—far more so than the slender purse of Adams would allow. The salary of $9000 a year was the same as that he had earned when he was minister to Prussia. But St. Petersburg was then the gaudiest court in Europe, where

Signing the Treaty of Ghent with Great Britain

Louisa Catherine Adams

Painting of John Quincy Adams by John Singleton Copley

Birthplace of the Adams' in Quincy, Massachusetts

President John Quincy Adams

John Quincy Adams, United States Congressman

John Quincy Adams suffers fatal stroke in House of Representatives

counts and dukes dined from plates of solid gold and held parties that never seemed to end.

Adams could not afford it, and he said as much. Worse, Louisa Adams could not even have the gowns she needed for some of these affairs, and was forced to plead illness sometimes to avoid embarrassment.

On one occasion during his stay, Adams encountered the Emperor on the street, and the Czar of all the Russias stopped him for a chat. Was he going to take a house in the country for the long, hot summer? the Emperor asked. Adams replied that he was not, but he did so briefly, in strained tones.

Was it a problem of finances, the Emperor wanted to know.

Adams admitted that it was. The Emperor endorsed his view that he ought not to live beyond his means.

Adams did continue to live within his means, although it was most difficult. Friends offered him loans, but he refused them, feeling that he had no right to mortgage his future while on a government mission overseas.

During this period the most magnificent embassy in St. Petersburg was that of Napoleon's envoy, the Duc de Vicence, Ambassador Caulaincourt. His official expenses were a million rubles a year (about $350,000). Even the Dutch minister spent about $18,000 a year, and the Swedish minister spent more than $10,000 a year.

As Minister Plenipotentiary, John Quincy Adams received a salary that was second only to that of the President of the United States. How could one explain to an economy-minded Congress that it was not enough? Even the Secretary of State, his chief, received only $5000 a year. Congress believed it had gone quite far enough in granting so much as $9000 to its ministers. There was nothing to be done but live frugally or go into debt.

Adams lived frugally—as frugally as he could, but he

had to have servants. He hired a steward, a cook, two scullions, a porter, two footmen, a janitor, a coachman and postillion, a valet, a personal maid, a house maid and a laundry maid. Those servants who were married brought their families to live in the house, too. Adams had to feed and support them, and they made off with food and his wines.

After a few weeks of this, Adams took strong action. He fired the cook and hired a caterer to bring in dinners from outside at seven dollars a day.

He wrote home about this problem, and his mother took it upon herself to write to James Madison and ask him to order John Quincy Adams to come home. Madison was not inclined to order his Minister thus, fortunately for Adams' future, but he did send Adams papers which would allow him to come home if he wished. And he proposed to appoint Adams to the United States Supreme Court if he wanted to return from this most difficult assignment.

But John Quincy Adams did not care that much for the law as a way of life. He liked his work, and why should he not? He had been preparing for such work almost all his life, and his most effective labors in the United States Senate had been concerned with foreign affairs. It was in this field that all senators had listened to Adams, whether they detested his personal politics or not. As a diplomat, Adams was an expert.

He refused the appointment to the Supreme Court, thus throwing over casually a career that thousands of lesser men would have considered to be the apex of their lives. He resigned himself to accepting a reputation for stinginess, and he settled down to life in St. Petersburg on a level he could afford.

Despite the French Ambassador's thousand dollar dinners, Adams was not detested or looked down upon in St. Petersburg. The others of the diplomatic colony seemed to

understand that the American minister was the victim of
his government's parsimony, and they made every allowance for his failures to reciprocate in entertainment. Nor
was the Emperor annoyed.

Actually, the plea of poverty made Adams' life considerably easier in one respect. He did not like the "irregular-
ity" and "dissipation" of social life in the Russian capital.
Parties began late at night and continued until the middle
hours of morning sometimes. He preferred to read, to study
Russian with the aid of a French-Russian dictionary, to
engage in his writings, his translations, and his other solitary work. He wanted to visit museums and libraries. The
release from social engagements allowed him to do these
things, and yet without acquiring a reputation as a boor.

Louisa fared worse. She did not like St. Petersburg. She
never learned the language well, and she was ill much of
the time because of the harsh climate.

But Adams was determined to remain in St. Petersburg,
and remain he did, even as Emperor Napoleon turned on
his brother emperor, Alexander, and began the march on
Moscow in 1812. America was at war, too, with Great Britain, and the major issue was impressment of American seamen by British war vessels. The *Chesapeake* incident was
a part of it. So was the British blockade of all Napoleonic
Europe.

Oddly enough, the British prime minister who was responsible for much of this policy, Spenser Perceval, was
assassinated in the spring of 1812, and on June 25 the new
government repealed the British acts which had been a
cause of strain between England and the United States.

But the British change in tactics came too late. The ob-
noxious policy had been in effect too long, and it had become a major political issue within the United States. On
June 18, 1812 a fiery group of nationalists in Congress

pushed through a declaration of war. The British action of a week later made no difference. The die was already cast.

Almost as soon as the war had begun, efforts were made by the Russian government to bring about a peace. The Russians were at war with France, and they feared that the United States would ally itself with France because France was at war with Britain.

Count Rumiantzov, the Russian Foreign Minister, began to make offers to mediate the dispute. Meanwhile, although Henry Clay and other fire-eaters had favored the war with England, Daniel Webster and most of the people of New England detested that war. Further, when the Americans launched military campaigns against Canada and Florida, they failed miserably. The failure brought shame to officials in Washington. President Madison leapt at the Russian offer to mediate and appointed two more ambassadors to come to Russia and serve with John Quincy Adams as a negotiating team. They were Albert Gallatin, the Secretary of the Treasury, and Senator James Bayard of Delaware.

The British government never did want this war with America, and Britain offered to negotiate, but not to mediate through a third party. The United States was equally ready to negotiate directly, for the War of 1812, which began so bravely had proved to be both ignoble and unnecessary from the American point of view. Once it was learned that the British had removed the cause almost at the same time that the war began, the position of the war group crumbled rapidly.

But all these negotiations and reversals of position took time. The peace commissioners arrived in St. Petersburg in the summer of 1813 and sat around restlessly for six months before they finally learned of Britain's decision to negotiate but not to mediate.

Their position was most awkward. They had no official standing at all until the British decided what they would do, and although the Czar received them, he did so in an informal and unofficial manner.

The entertainment of the two prominent Americans posed constant problems for St. Petersburg's diplomatic colony. To entertain them officially would be to court the displeasure of Great Britain, and with a war against France on their hands, the Russians wanted none of that. Nor did other diplomats of other lands want such problems. The British took the position that the men did not exist.

For months the negotiating team wrangled at long distance over the place where peace talks might be held, and eventually compromised on Ghent, in Belgium, or what was then called Dutch Flanders. President Madison appointed a new peace commission, adding to the three early members the names of Henry Clay, who was then Speaker of the House of Representatives, and Jonathan Russell, a rising young diplomat. Adams was the chairman of the American delegation to the Ghent talks.

In the spring of 1814 the peace commissioners traveled to Ghent and took bachelor apartments at the Hotel Lovendeghem, Adams leaving his wife and son behind in St. Petersburg.

One of Adams' major problems as a human being showed itself in the very beginning of this association. The other four commissioners were inclined to sit after dinner and "drink bad wine and smoke cigars," Adams noted. He found that drinking bad wine was hard on his health, and he was certain that the amount of liquor Henry Clay drank was hard on Clay's health too. Adams also had given up smoking at the age of 45, and now did not have much patience with those who wanted to waste their time thus.

Nor did Adams approve of the habits of the others. They

spent their time in billiard rooms and coffee houses. He
spent his time in museums and on long walks and in book-
shops. He arose at dawn to read his Bible, and on one such
rising, he heard a card party ending in Clay's room which
joined his own.

Clay was characteristically open and blunt about these
differences. The matter came to a head when Adams took
a separate table at dinner and ate in solitary contemplation
while the other four Americans sat nearby. Clay said it was
silly, and pushed Adams into joining them.

He did join them with good grace, and thereafter they
all ate together, even bringing in their secretaries and
other members of their staffs.

The Americans represented different backgrounds and
regions and points of view, but they managed over a period
of months to hold together a united front in their negotiations with the British.

The Treaty of Ghent ended, as did the War of 1812, apparently without very much having been accomplished by
either side. But the truth was a bit different from that. The
British were winning the War of 1812 in 1814 when these
negotiations began. Had Britain not been involved so
deeply in military operations in Europe, she would have
pursued the war, and the course of American history might
have been much different. For among the items the British
wanted to discuss at Ghent were the establishment of terri-
torial lines for the Indian allies of Britain and the revision
of the American-Canadian boundary lines. What Britain
wanted to do was push down the Hudson river and cut off
the westward movement of the American nation across the
continent. Britain would have liked also to have taken pos-
session of the Louisiana Purchase territory, and to have
the Mississippi made an international waterway which

would give England a high road running along the borders of the United States.

One by one the major issues disappeared. The Duke of Wellington conquered Napoleon at Bordeau, and the question of impressment of American sailors became academic. With the end of Britain's naval war, there would be no need for a huge navy and an increasing supply of sailors. The Indian allies of Britain made separate peace with the Americans and declared war on the British! That put an end to the Indian question. But the question of adjusting the boundary between Canada and the United States persisted and was difficult to decide.

The British abandoned their original demand—that territory which now includes the states of Wisconsin, Michigan, Illinois, part of Indiana and Ohio should all be given to the Indians outright. In the end the Americans held out for a treaty which returned America to the status she enjoyed before the war. In other words, practically having lost the war, the Americans managed to secure a treaty which cost the nation nothing in territory, at a time when the British wanted some of that territory. They managed it because Britain's attention was focused on Europe.

Now came two events in America which were to have bearing on the affairs of John Quincy Adams in the future. The Treaty of Ghent was signed on December 24, and sent home as soon as it was ratified by the British government. But news traveled slowly in those days, and the peace treaty was not received in Washington until February 14. In the meantime, two weeks after the signing of the treaty in England, Andrew Jackson had defeated the British decisively in the Battle of New Orleans. Washington learned of this victory February 11.

These twin pieces of news, a victory in battle and an honorable peace, brought the complete collapse of the *Essex Junto.* The Essex men had met in convention at Hartford, Connecticut to demand peace at any price and the removal of the men who had brought war to America. The news destroyed their every argument and their every hope of achieving power or even respectability. The *Essex Junto,* the implacable enemy of John Quincy Adams, was destroyed.

☆ ☆ ☆

CHAPTER 5

Affairs of State

ONCE THE Treaty of Ghent was worked out and it became apparent that peace would come, John Quincy Adams sent for his wife and son in St. Petersburg. After an amazing ride across country in Eastern Europe, nearly mobbed at one point because pro-French villagers and French troops thought they were enemy Russians, the Adams family arrived in Paris.

Soon, they were involved in a whirl of Parisian entertainments. Adams indulged an old passion for the theater, attending performances nearly every evening. He was presented at court to Louis XVIII, a few days before Louis went flying eastward out of the country as Napoleon returned from Elba, to which he had moved after his abdication.

Adams watched, an interested spectator, as Napoleon rushed through the Hundred Days of his second surge to power, only to be defeated at Waterloo and finally taken as a prisoner of war to lonely St. Helena to live only six years more in restless captivity. Louis XVIII came home again, but Adams' attention was now elsewhere for he had been chosen minister plenipotentiary to Great Britain, and he watched the last part of the Napoleonic drama from London, not from Paris.

In London, Adams, along with Henry Clay and Albert Gallatin again participated in the drafting of a trade agree-

ment with the British. But his real mission, after the others
went home, was to bring about a true reconciliation between the United States and England. For actually, although the Revolution had begun nearly forty years before,
the countries had never truly settled down to mutual acceptance of each other.

Adams was happier, and Louisa Adams was far happier
in London than they ever had been in St. Petersburg. The
level of expense was very high in London, too, but for quite
a different reason. After peace came, the demands of Adams'
countrymen on him became great. Young Americans began
traveling to Europe as a part of their "cultural education."
Their first port of call, almost inevitably, was London, and
there they expected the American Minister to go out of his
way to show them courtesies. Such courtesies cost money.

Adams and his wife moved to a country house a few
miles outside London. This gave them a place to escape the
constant round of entertainment in the London social
world, and also to maintain themselves without the crush-
ing expenses they would have incurred in London. The
boys who had remained in America joined them there
and went to school. Adams had them taught fencing and
undertook to teach them to shoot a pistol himself, but the
pistol kicked back in his hand and made it impossible for
him to write for several weeks.

The London interlude lasted until 1817. Adams kept in
close contact with his mother and father by letter, and did
not complain when they still pushed and pulled at him as
though he were a child. His mother once secured the appointment of one of her grandsons, a nephew of Adams, as
a secretary to the Minister to London. She had gone directly
to the Secretary of State and the President, without con-
sulting her son. He swallowed the appointment ruefully,
but was pleasantly surprised when his nephew turned out
to be an excellent secretary.

Old John Adams and his wife wanted their son to come home. Among other matters, the former President was eager to have his son undertake the editing and arrangement of his presidential papers for the public. Adams also planned to publish his own memoirs one day, based upon his diaries. But if he were to come home, how would he earn his living and what profession would he pursue?

It was apparent to all that he had no great love for the law as his father had. His political career in elective office had been blighted by his independence, and while the *Essex Junto* had now disappeared from the Massachusetts scene, the memory of Adams' independence lingered on in many places.

No, it would take some stroke of luck or genius to bring Adams into elective political life once again. Barring either, Adams remained in London, waiting and watching.

Then, when James Monroe was elected President of the United States in 1816, Monroe decided to make Adams his Secretary of State. The word first came to John Adams the father, who informed his son that the appointment would be forthcoming and advised him to accept it without hesitation.

There was little real doubt in Adams' mind when the offer came. Among other considerations was his desire to continue in public office. And here, almost within his grasp it seemed, was first the leadership of the nation in foreign affairs, and secondly, in good time, the Presidency of the United States. This last aspect of the appointment was in the minds of all, because, since the beginning of American independence, the road to the Presidency had led through the office of Secretary of State. That cabinet member was heir-apparent to the President. He was privy to the President's most important decisions of policy, and he was the man who learned best from the President how the affairs of the nation ought to be run—at least in times like those of the first quarter of the nineteenth century, when political differences, hot as they might be, still involved men who were basically of gentle birth and gentle education.

The appointment was made, and John Quincy Adams came home to assume the highest office he had yet attained.

Why was Adams chosen—a man who had been out of the country for many years?

That was one of the major reasons for his selection. James Monroe found him eminently suitable because he had been out of the nation for two presidential terms, and thus had not engaged in any of the politicking of the period. Furthermore, the other most likely candidate for the job, Henry Clay, was a southerner, as was Monroe. The northeastern states would have looked with the greatest jealousy on the appointment of Clay to this post, and although Clay wanted the State Department and no other post, he did not get it, largely for this reason.

In the summer of 1817 the Adams family came home. Early on the morning of August 6, the ship came within sight of the famous highlands of Navesink on the New Jersey coast. A pilot schooner pulled up alongside, and the pilot was taken aboard the sailing ship at six in the morning. At one in the afternoon, having been driven by a light breeze, the ship had passed through the Narrows between Staten Island and Brooklyn and was pulled up to the wharf in New York City. The long voyage was ended, but another voyage was begun.

Adams was given a magnificent welcome by the leaders of New York. John Jacob Astor came to escort him to a dinner given for the new Secretary of State at Tammany Hall. He met Governor DeWitt Clinton there. Having paid his obeisances to politics, Adams escaped for a bit, and in the company of John Trumbull, the artist, he went on a tour of New York's museums and art galleries with the same delight he had shown in touring similar institutions in St. Petersburg, Paris, and London.

As always, Adams arose early in the morning, said his prayers, made his toilet, read his Bible for an hour, and then settled down at his desk to write in his journal. On the morning of August 15, he followed his usual course and continued until his sons came knocking at his door to announce that it was almost seven o'clock.

Seven o'clock! That was the hour at which the steamboat would, leave for Boston. Instead of occupying himself in intellectual exercise, Adams should have been up at five, packing and making ready to take the boat.

They hurried as quickly as they could, but when their carriage arrived at the Fulton street wharf, they discovered that the steamboat waited for no one, not even a secretary of state. They had missed the boat by five minutes.

Adams then, had his first rude encounter with the industrial age on which America was embarking. The quiet, gentlemanly days of the past—when affairs proceeded without haste—were passing into history. Adams saw more of the change when he arrived in Boston, after a trip by sailing packet. In eight years the city had burst forth into a glorious mass of new buildings. Beacon Hill had been demolished, which he regretted. But for the rest, he could see nothing but change for the better.

There was change in the political atmosphere of Boston, too. Adams had left the city eight years before with the catcalls of the Federalists ringing in his ears. Now he was given a testimonial dinner at the Exchange Coffee House, escorted by his father, former President of the United States. Generals, chief justices, governors, and university presidents crowded around to wish him well and shake his hand.

Federalism as a political movement was dead. To be sure, there were still men alive and active who called themselves

Federalists. Their major precept was a belief that a "governing class" continued to exist and that privilege along with background and education should be pre-requisite for high office in government. But the Federalists had made the political mistake of turning against their own government during the War of 1812. It was one thing to oppose the war, but quite another to say that the British were right—and that was the position adopted by the ultra-Federalists. It destroyed them in the end.

At this point in American history, there really was only one party movement, the Republican movement, which was showing signs of becoming the Democratic party that we know today. However the signs were not yet fully developed. James Monroe, the President, was opposed to political parties in principle, as was John Adams. Monroe felt that in breaking away from the old world the Revolutionaries of 1776 had destroyed the party system. He saw in the downfall of the Federalists over the war issue the proof of his argument.

Four-fifths of the people of the United States believed in the principles of the Republican party, but there were beginnings of new kinds of factionalism, too. The factionalism was buried for the moment in surprised pleasure at the adoption by Monroe of some old Federalist principles: support of a standing army and a navy and help for American manufacturers. In the latter issue lay the seeds of the tariff question which was to create political parties later on when manufacturing had become more important.

Other factional differences began to appear even in this so-called "Era of Good Feeling" when the South and West began to gain population at the expense of the East. Those who moved west, in particular, were a hardy breed of pioneers with no time or place for class distinctions on the frontier. And in the cities, the working men who lived in the same neighborhoods began to discover that they had similar problems with employers, and with their affairs, whether they worked as mattress makers or in the shipyards. No organized labor existed, nor anything truly like it, but there were stirrings of interest in the laboring group.

On the surface James Monroe's policies seemed absolutely correct, and there was no political cleavage in the government. But in his selection of the cabinet, Monroe had denied Henry Clay the one position he sought—Secretary of State. Clay was offered the War Department and refused it, whereupon it went to John C. Calhoun. That left the West unrepresented in the Monroe cabinet, and left Henry Clay, champion of the West, outside too. It was an error that would not be immediately fatal, but it would strengthen the feeling of westerners that they had no place in the government at Washington.

On September 20 Adams and his wife arrived in Washington where he would take up his duties as Secretary of State. President Monroe had moved back into the White House, which had been repaired after having been burned by the British during the war. Washington was still a miserable little city, not in any way comparable to the capitals in which Adams had labored for so long. But he did not seem to mind. When in Washington his whole effort was directed to the art of government, and he did not complain about the demands on him nearly so much as in other lands, where social parties, in particular, always aroused complaints because he was being dragged away from his studies.

President Monroe and Secretary of State Adams made a remarkably effective team in the conduct of American foreign relations. Adams was a workhorse. He was bright and sharp and an excellent organizer of the detail of the State Department. When he arrived in Washington, he learned that routing and filing of documents were so carelessly handled that even one treaty had become lost somewhere. No one knew how many important letters and documents from statesmen abroad had remained unread or could no longer be found for reference. Adams changed this by establishing a tight system in the State Department. Soon, although the United States spent less on management of foreign affairs than the British spent on espionage for the foreign office, the American foreign service began to assume a professional aspect.

Adams was held in check in some other ways by President Monroe, who was an excellent administrator and a strong executive. Adams did not run American foreign affairs. The President of the United States ran them, as he was supposed to, and Adams was his steward and advisor.

As Secretary of State, Adams dealt with hundreds of problems that seemed most important then, and were important, although history has dulled them for us. For example, the question of protocol disturbed the capital for months. Mrs. Monroe never called on anyone. Mrs. Madison had called on everyone. Mrs. Adams, wife of the Secretary of State, called on the wives of foreign ambassadors only after they had called on her. And the wives of the ambassadors greatly resented this, going in the end to Mrs. Monroe to complain. Mrs. Adams stuck to her guns.

The Spanish Ambassador was much upset because South America had rebelled, a number of nations had been formed, and new ministers had come to Washington where they were courteously accepted. The Spanish Ambassador was subjected to a number of mischievous harassments. His house was broken into. He received threatening messages. He complained to Secretary Adams that Spain was being mistreated in Washington.

Important issues came before Adams as well. Amity with England proceeded to grow splendidly despite the presence

in Washington of a British Minister whom Adams did not
totally respect. Henry Clay, piqued at having been left out
of the cabinet as heir-apparent to the Presidency, began to
stir up an opposition movement in Congress. Opposition
to Adams also arose in several other areas, for since he was
Secretary of State, it was generally accepted that he was the
men to beat for the presidential nomination after Monroe's
second term in office.

This was also the era of the Missouri Compromise and of
the concentration of the government on internal improvements. There were dozens of great issues in these eight
years, many of which would affect John Quincy Adams
later, but there was no single matter that concerned him
more than the Seminole War of 1818 and its aftermath.

In 1812 the British had built a fort on the Apalachicola
river in East Florida. The territory nominally belonged to
Spain, but again it was one of those matters that had been
left inconveniently undecided in the Louisiana Purchase.
Florida had been mentioned, but scarcely more than that,
since the matter seemed unimportant at the time.

When the War of 1812 ended, the fort and the area
around it became a refuge for runaway slaves and bad-
tempered Indians. In 1816 an American military expedi-
tion was dispatched to destroy the fort and did so. Other
Indian groups were pursued into territory that was defi-
nitely held by Spain.

In 1817 General Andrew Jackson, the hero of New Orleans, was given command of the forces in the area. Jackson
was a man of action, and he took action now. He wrote a
letter to President Monroe stating that if it could be sig-
nified to him unofficially in any way that the control of the
Florida peninsula would be helpful to American interests,
it could be accomplished in sixty days. The President did
not reply to the letter, and General Jackson took that si-

lence to mean that he could do as he wished. He began to march.

In the spring of 1818, as John Quincy Adams was talking to Spain's Minister Luis de Onis, the word came that Jackson had captured the Spanish fort of St. Mark's. Adams did not seem to be too much disturbed. Perhaps he felt it gave the American government a wedge with which to force a rapid settlement of the Florida question.

But Jackson continued to move. He captured Pensacola next, and with its capture, he also executed two Englishmen when a court-martial found them guilty of aiding the Indians. There was some belief that the verdict of the military court was ordered by Jackson.

The Jackson actions caused a furor in the United States. President Monroe and all the members of the cabinet, except Adams, took the position that Jackson had exceeded his orders and had caused serious embarrassment to the government. It was a natural enough position, since Monroe had already been in disagreement with Jackson over the General's refusal to accept a direct order given to one of his staff by the War Department. (Jackson took the position that the government could give *him* orders and he would give them to the men under his command.)

Adams, and Adams alone, supported Jackson's actions. Secretary of War Calhoun seemed the most visibly affected and the most angry, probably because he felt that Jackson was again defying his superiors.

Adams argued in Jackson's behalf during several heated cabinet meetings. In Congress, the House condemned Jackson's conduct. Henry Clay led a group which proposed a measure of censure against the General. A Senate committee investigated and reported its disapproval of Jackson's actions.

Calhoun and another cabinet member wanted some action taken against Jackson—perhaps removal from command or censure by the President. But President Monroe was quick to realize that public opinion was rallying behind Jackson's action, particularly in the West, and he was very sensitive to western opinion at this time. The public, more than any cabinet officer except Adams, seemed to realize that the Jackson sortie had strengthened America's position vis-à-vis Spain. So nothing was done, except that the captured territory finally was handed back to Spain, but only for a short time. Adams succeeded in securing the Florida territory outright by assuming five million dollars of the claims of its citizens against Spain and renouncing claims to Texas.

Adams had time during these years to pursue some of his own interests. He traveled to New York and visited John Trumbull again to look over Trumbull's painting of the signing of the Declaration of Independence. Adams, a man of vigorous taste, did not like the painting very much. His love of the exact brought him to complain about the lettering on books on the President's table. They were titled Locke and Sidney, after two notable writers on the affairs of men. Adams said those books would have been read at home, but would not have been brought into the meeting by the revolutionaries who were preparing the Declaration. He advised the artist to change the lettering to "journals."

Shortly after the Jackson argument, Henry Clay decided to retire from politics for a time. He said he had to go home to Kentucky to repair his personal fortunes. Before Clay left Washington, he called at Adams' office on business. One thing he wanted was a special payment for his work in negotiating the commercial agreement with Britain in 1815. Adams told Clay then that he did not think anything could be done without a special appropriation from Congress. Adams was not particularly sympathetic in the conversation. Later, in his journal, he was sharp and critical of Clay for seeking private gain from public trust, and noted that he suspected that Clay had refrained from attacking him recently in hope that Adams would support the claim.

In the summary of the conversation, given in his diary, Adams showed his own personal characteristics more than those of Henry Clay. He was quick to criticize Clay but he conveniently forgot that when he had returned from his mission to Holland and Prussia, and when he needed money to establish himself in law practice in Boston, John Quincy Adams had come, hat in hand to the national capital, seeking payment of what he thought was due him from the government.

➤ Adams recognized Clay as a powerful and successful politician. On the occasion of his retirement, Clay had come to him, and from the Adams report of the conversation, Clay seems to have come seeking friendship. Adams was incapable of giving friendship, and he met Clay's gesture with the suspicion which accompanied all his dealings with men outside his own family group.

It was strange that a man who could be so cold to outsiders could be so loving in the family, and particularly to his mother and father, whom he looked up to all his life. It was true that he did not have any great love for his wife. He regarded his marriage as "satisfactory", not as the great partnership some other men felt in marriage—men like Henry Clay, for example.

When Adams' mother died, during his tenure as Secretary of State, John Quincy was deeply affected. He wrote in his diary that he left the office that day and went home. Only a mighty blow would have sent him away from his work. He also wrote of his mother's virtues, and never in his writings did he make serious complaint about the overbearing nature of either of his parents. He would not have stood for such in any other person.

He stood for very little variation from his own standards of behavior from any members of his family. He wrote alarmingly harsh letters to his sons. When one of them failed to come within the first half of his class at Harvard, John Quincy Adams refused to allow the boy permission to come home for the Christmas holidays. When another son was expelled from Harvard altogether with other rebellious members of his class, Adams never forgave the boy.

Adams was a harsh man, as some said of others—"all brain and no heart"—but as such he was an extremely effective Secretary of State. He knew more about European affairs and had more experience in diplomacy than any foreign envoy in the capital. He could hold his own end of any conversation on intellectual subjects, and aroused in European nations a respect for American policy that had not been apparent before. So it was obvious, as the end of James Monroe's second term as President of the United States drew near, that John Quincy Adams was in an extremely favorable position to become President of the United States.

A few years before, one might have said that his succession would have been nearly automatic. But in the past eight years, a great number of changes had taken place in America. No longer was there total respect for men of culture and family as such. Others who had gone on to the frontiers of the expanding nation had created new legends which seized the public imagination every bit as much as did the stories of George Washington, the Massachusetts patriots of the Revolution, and the landed gentry of the entire nation who had led the rebellion against England. There was a definite broadening of the basis of American society, and the two heroic figures in this movement were Andrew Jackson and Henry Clay, political enemies but both popular figures. There was no mistaking Adams' ambition now, although Adams had never been entirely frank about it. He wanted desperately to be President of the United States just as he had always truly wanted that position. And, despite his many defects of character as a politician and despite his personal coldness, it was obvious in 1824 that he had a very good chance of becoming first executive.

☆ ☆ ☆

CHAPTER 6

The Election of 1824

THE CAMPAIGN for the election of 1824 began almost as soon as President Monroe was inaugurated in his second term in office in the spring of 1821. This was an unusual situation and an indication of the changes that were occurring in American society.

Early in the year the newspapers which favored various candidates began to push their cause vigorously. These were the days of an extremely partisan press. Adams had had much experience with that press and its excesses in his long period in public office and did not pay too much attention to it. Nor did the other candidates or the general public, for that matter, for when the newspapers shrilled about the virtues of one candidate or the deviltries of another they were usually addressing an audience that was already convinced.

The principal candidate, insofar as effort was concerned, was William Crawford, the big, easy-moving Secretary of the Treasury. He was accused by his enemies of plotting to seize the nomination from the time he became Secretary of the Treasury. But Crawford suffered from a situation that has plagued politicians both before and since that time. He was so obviously a candidate, for so long, that the public tired of his name before it came time to choose a man to succeed James Monroe. That did not stop Crawford and his supporters, however.

John Quincy Adams continued in office as Secretary of State, and continued to do the same diligent job of organizing the foreign service and supervising foreign relations. Although in his fifties, he took up swimming seriously and in the summer of 1823, was often to be found in the afternoons swimming in the Potomac with friends, sometimes for as long as an hour and a half without touching ground or bottom. Adams approached swimming as he did nearly everything else in life, industriously, without humor, and with great skill. He became an excellent swimmer.

During the early 1820's there seemed to be no basic political differences within the nation, but this was not really the case. The country was beginning to split along political lines, and certain realignments were already visible.

For one thing, Virginia was no longer the most populous state in the Union, which it had been for many years. New York now claimed that honor, and in New York the political organization known as Tammany Hall had seized power in the largest city in the state—New York City.

Another sign of change was to be seen in New England. Domination by the Congregational church was ending there. It had already ended in all the states but Massachusetts, and in this period it was to end in Massachusetts too, and the question of religious affiliation was to make no difference in the holding of public office.

The West was growing rapidly, and the westerners were becoming alienated ever more from the eastern states. Factional disputes were arising over the emphasis to be placed on internal improvements, the tariff, the question of national finance and the handling of national currency, and foreign affairs. But the important factionalism of the period was not concerned with issues so much as men. The men involved were Crawford, Adams, John C. Calhoun, Henry Clay, and Andrew Jackson.

In Congress each man had his own group of supporters, and so ardent did they become, as the second Monroe term slipped away, that outsiders claimed this Seventeenth American Congress had little on its mind but politicking —this in a nation where the fondest hope of the President was that partisan politics had been put aside forever!

President Monroe was careful to refrain from any sign of favoritism to one candidate or another. He accepted the principle of two-term rule—that is, the idea laid down first by Washington, that no man ought to serve more than twice in the highest executive office in the land. John Quincy Adams disagreed with that principle. He believed that because of this rule the President, once elected, would be spending all his time in a whirlwind of politics. Adams retained some of his family feeling for a privileged class, and because of this feeling, he was not worried about the possibility that one man might build a political machine and retain power indefinitely. He felt that only the proper kind of man might be able to perpetuate himself in office, and the idea did not bother him.

Adams was totally opposed to any kind of politics or electioneering. He believed, seriously, that the office of President would unerringly seek the proper man for the job. Inherent in this belief was Adams' faith in himself, and his sureness that he was the proper man for the job and the logical successor to James Monroe. He particularly hated William H. Crawford—perhaps because Crawford was so successful a politician, which to Adams meant "intriguer."

As the year 1821 wore on, the campaigns of the major candidates speeded up. Calhoun was a young man, not yet forty, and he was a serious contender for the Presidency, although he was adept at hiding his feelings. He told Adams that he thought the next President ought to be a northerner, since the Virginians had dominated the Presidency

in its early years. (Adams' father had been the only northern man to hold the office.) But Calhoun was not totally
sincere. He was courting Adams in order to conceal his own
ambition. While he spoke of supporting Adams, he was
really trying to win northern allegiance to his own candi-
dacy.

As the campaigning wore on, and Adams learned Calhoun's true position, he grew more and more annoyed with
Calhoun and so indicated in his private diary.

Adams apparently did not consider Andrew Jackson to
be a serious contender for the office of President in 1824,
for Adams was most friendly to Jackson during this period.
In fact, Adams again came to Jackson's support in a serious
matter when other members of the cabinet sided against
the General.

Yet, even had Adams known that Jackson would be a
contender, the Secretary of State was not an ignoble man.
On the contrary, he and Andrew Jackson shared some important qualities of greatness. Both had performed great
public services to the nation over long periods of years. Both
were unselfish men, in terms of public service. Both held a
vision of American greatness unshared by many of the men
around them.

Adams admired Andrew Jackson as much as he admired
any other man. In his biography of John Quincy Adams,
Bennett Champ Clark says that Adams admired Jackson
more than any men but his father and George Washington.

The candidacies of the various men were pushed by their
supporters in Congress. This put Adams and Jackson at
some disadvantage, for Clay and Calhoun were great congressional figures, and Crawford had served with distinction
in many posts.

Adams was at further disadvantage because of his unfortunate manner. Few men denied that he was a brilliant

leader and a brilliant statesman. But he alienated people
almost without trying. Many representatives and senators
were annoyed because Mrs. Adams would not come to call.
Adams placed the figure of angry congressmen at one-third
the total in Washington in those days.

But offsetting this was the pleasant practice the Adamses
maintained of holding formal receptions on each Tuesday
evening. In those days they kept a mansion on F street,
across from the present site of the National Press Club in
downtown Washington. There Mrs. Adams held court, and
while much of Washington society said that these were very
dull affairs and that Adams had no talent for mixing in society, at least this social gesture set aside some of the criticism of Adams as unfriendly.

In small groups Adams could be and was charming to
others. Martin Van Buren, the suave New York gentleman, said that John Quincy Adams was the most charming
and interesting table companion he knew.

But in public, it was another story and a sad one.

Champ Clark noticed that in one country visit Adams
showed just how awkward a politician he was. He did not
kiss babies and he did not shake hands well or slap backs.
He could not even carry on a reasonable conversation with
an unknown voter.

One day during the campaign, Clark said, Adams came
upon an old farmer who was delighted to see him.

"Mr. Adams," he said. "My wife, when she was a gal, lived
in your father's family; you were then a little boy, and she
has often combed your head."

Adams was unimpressed.

"Well, I suppose she combs yours now," he said to the
farmer, thus throwing away at least one vote that day.

But Adams was not as poor a politician as that story
would make him seem to be. At the Fourth of July celebra-

tion in Washington in 1821, John Quincy Adams arose to make the oration. In his hand he held the original copy of the Declaration of Independence (which was kept in the State Department in those days). He read the document before a cheering crowd—and he read it well, for had he not been professor of oratory and rhetoric at Harvard? As was then the custom in American politics, Adams "twisted the Lion's tail"—that is, he assailed Great Britain and King George over and over again, while the people cheered.

And in 1824, on the eve of the real campaign for the Presidency, John Quincy Adams held a great ball in honor of Andrew Jackson. The occasion was the anniversary of the Battle of New Orleans and the Treaty of Ghent—at which these two different men had served their nations so well. The ball was actually held on January 6, 1824, and it was a great success of the Washington social season. General Jackson appeared and was gracious throughout the evening. So was John Quincy Adams. Calhoun and Henry Clay were there, too, in the blue coats, high white chokers and silk stockings of the day. The affair was marred only when General Winfield Scott's pocket was picked of $600—but no one could blame the host or the guest of honor for that unfortunate incident.

Adams was a brilliant man; no one questioned that or his fitness to become President of the United States. He had been a party to the formulation of the Monroe Doctrine, that most important plank of the American foreign policy platform of the nineteenth and early twentieth centuries. Some said that Adams was responsible for much of the wording of the Monroe Doctrine, but that is not the important part of it. President James Monroe was chief officer of the United States and the praise or censure for various policies belonged to him and not to his subordinates. Adams' work was important in the Monroe Doctrine, which warned European nations against trying to colonize Latin America or bringing European power into the waters of the Americas. It was an important policy, and while President Monroe deserves all credit for it, the skill with which it was drawn depended in large part on Adams' great experience and diplomatic genius.

But foreign policy was not to be the deciding factor in the election of 1824. Bitter as the campaign was to become, it was not to be decided by issues at all, but by a strange form of personal politics that was unparalleled in American presidential history.

As far as John Quincy Adams was concerned, his ability to attract votes from New York would determine his position. Clay and Jackson were sure to attract the West and much of the South. Crawford, a slave-holder, hoped to attract the South, and more, to win by engineering his selection by the old caucus system. The election of 1824 was notable, however, for the downfall of the caucus system. At the Congressional caucus held that year, only 66 of the 261 Representatives appeared, and although these unanimously nominated Crawford and Albert Gallatin for President and Vice-President, no one paid very much attention. The number of men voting was too small to affect the outcome of the contest in the nation. Not long afterward, Crawford suffered a stroke and almost complete disablement. He was effectively put out of the race.

Martin Van Buren in New York controlled a political machine known as the Albany Regency. He wanted Crawford nominated and elected, and did all that he could to bring that situation about. Simultaneously DeWitt Clinton was opposing the Albany Regency, which further confused affairs in New York State.

At this time, without Adams' knowledge or even understanding of the political situation in New York, a young

man named Thurlow Weed took charge of the Adams campaign. Weed did not have any particular reputation as a
politician then. He was only a young reporter on a Rochester newspaper and had recently served as a lobbyist for a
group of bankers who wanted to establish a new bank in
Rochester. This work had brought him into close contact
with politicians and had showed him a new field which at-
tracted him.

He did not know Adams, and he had not even been in
correspondence with Adams. Adams would never have paid
any attention to this young man even if he had written to
him.

That did not bother Weed. He was interested in politics
for the sake of politics. While he believed that John Quincy
Adams would make the best President, he also wanted to
get into the political fighting in New York State. This
candidate, who refused to seek the office, and thus had no
political organization, was made to order for Thurlow
Weed's purposes.

Just before the legislature was to meet and decide whom
it would support for the Presidency, the Van Buren forces
made a serious political error. Governor Clinton had become most unpopular, so unpopular that he did not even
stand for reelection. After he was out of office the Van
Buren forces removed him from the Erie Canal commission to which he had been appointed, and where he was doing an excellent job.

This arbitrary political removal caused an eruption in
New York State, and a widespread demand for electoral
reform. In the confusion, Weed championed the cause of
Clinton, who then was triumphantly nominated for governor by the newly-formed People's party.

In the further confusion generated by all this political

warfare, the legislature met to nominate its candidate for President.

Under New York's election law then, the house and the senate each voted on an electoral ticket. If they did not agree on the same men they met in joint session and settled on one set of candidates.

That year the two houses disagreed, and in the compromise that followed, Weed brought about a meeting of the Clay and Adams men. They agreed to support a union ticket; they would send thirty Adams men and six Clay men to vote in the electoral college.

The election followed. When the Van Buren men knew they had been tricked, they threatened to break up the meeting. They were restrained, and the work was finished. Adams got his twenty-six votes from New York, which meant that he would poll enough in the Electoral College to throw the election into the House of Representatives, with his name on the list. Clay, however, was robbed. In the New York trade he had been cheated out of four votes, and it was by just four votes that Crawford's polling exceeded Clay's in the Electoral College.

So Henry Clay, who wanted desperately to be President of the United States, was defeated from consideration by almost a hair. According to the electoral rules, the three candidates who polled the highest number of votes would be put before the House of Representatives and a President chosen from among them. Andrew Jackson had polled 99 votes, Adams had 84, including the solid vote of New England, and Crawford had 41. John C. Calhoun, the sole candidate for the vice-presidency, polled 182 votes.

The election then rested in the palm of the hand of Henry Clay. It was odd. Had he managed to pull the extra votes in New York City, he would have been one of the

three candidates before the House of Representatives, and
almost surely would have been elected President, so high
was his standing in Congress. But he was not among the
three, so all he could do was control the selection of the President by his great influence.

The results of the election by the Electoral College were
known in mid-December. Thereafter the friends of the
three candidates began feverishly to cultivate Henry Clay.
Clay was amused, but not so amused that he failed to play
his role as a political genius.

In the past Clay had been engaged in conflict with both
John Quincy Adams and General Andrew Jackson. His
dislike of Adams as a person had roots back in the days of
the Ghent negotiations, when Adams had been so stand-
offish socially and so demanding as a negotiator representing basically a New England set of interests. The personal
question had arisen again when Adams was chosen Secretary of State by Monroe over Clay. But Clay also had engaged in controversy with General Jackson, and he particularly disliked Jackson's activities in Florida.

Crawford was out of it as far as Clay was concerned, because Crawford's health did not justify his even standing
for the office.

Clay knew that neither Jackson nor Adams liked him.
He had crossed swords with Adams in particular, during
the campaign just past. It had been a vile campaign in which
everything about all candidates was given the worst possible
coloration. Adams was subjected to complaints and innuen-
does about his "English" wife. Jonathan Russell, who had
been one of the Ghent negotiators so long ago, had published a letter which seemed to show that at Ghent, Adams
had been willing to surrender American rights on the Mississippi river in favor of fishing rights in Newfoundland wa-

ters. His intention was to destroy Adams with the westerners and southerners. Adams managed to find the original
letter in the government's files and proved that the Russell
letter was a forgery. He also showed himself to be a cam-
paigner who fought without giving or asking quarter, so
much so that his friends tried to tone him down lest he add
unfortunately to his reputation as a harsh figure.
Russell was ruined politically in this interchange, and more
heat was generated between Clay and Adams.

But when it came down to choosing between the two men
Clay was guided by practical politics.

If he chose Jackson, then in his middle forties, Clay
would be strengthening the position of a candidate who
could threaten his own political future. Furthermore, Jackson was a soldier, and Clay did not like the idea of soldiers
in political office. (Jackson was also United States Senator
from Tennessee at that point, but there was nothing Clay
could do about that.)

All three candidates sought Clay's support, more or less
openly. Jackson dined with Clay several times that winter.
Adams paid a courtesy call on Clay and his friend Congressman Robert Letcher. Later Letcher called at the State Department to discover Adams' sentiments toward Clay. Certainly Adams did not tell Letcher his secret feelings which
he confided only to his diary. He had no animosity to Clay,
he said. And Clay had no animosity to him, Letcher replied.

Thus it was that Clay decided to work for Adams for the
Presidency. Later, an embittered Andrew Jackson was to
charge that a deal had been made—Clay had traded his support on promise of high office from John Quincy Adams.
Yet this does not fit Adams' character, or Clay's, and it is
generally conceded by historians that the tale, once believed true, is a distortion of a complicated set of facts.

Nor did Clay's support automatically assure Adams of election to the Presidency. Andrew Jackson's supporters were far more enthusiastic about their man than Adams' supporters were about him. The Jackson men were believers in popular democracy. They came from the West, many of them, and they made up in fervor what they lacked in manners and political sagacity.

When it came right down to the day of election, February 9, there still was doubt as to the outcome, for the alignment of votes was such as to produce a very close election.

Almost until the last moment, several key men were undecided. Clay had taken control of the Adams forces, assisted by Daniel Webster, and he tried to bring these men into line. Among them was General Stephen Van Renssalaer, a member of an old, respected New York family.

General Van Renssalaer was committed to vote for William Crawford, who had not given up hope that he might be elected. More hopeful even than Crawford was Martin Van Buren, who had supported Crawford staunchly if not very successfully in New York, and who wanted to keep Adams out.

On the first ballot, General Van Renssalaer held control. If he cast his vote for Crawford or for Jackson, there could be no election winner and if a second ballot were necessary the alignment of forces might be changed.

General Van Renssalaer, according to Van Buren, went to the Capitol on the day of the election prepared to vote against Adams. He had been taken to see Adams by Clay a few days before the election in the House, but had not been convinced to vote for the Massachusetts man.

On arrival at the Capitol, General Van Renssalaer was stopped by Clay and Webster, who together used their most persuasive powers to change his mind. They painted a picture of government disorganization, which, they said, must certainly follow if the House of Representatives failed to elect a President. It was his duty, they urged, to prevent such a chaotic eventuality.

General Van Renssalaer went to his seat, disturbed. He did not know quite what to do. While waiting to vote, he dropped his head on the desk and asked for Divine Guidance.

When he opened his eyes, Van Buren said in his autobiography, the General saw before him a piece of paper with the name of John Quincy Adams on it—a ballot marked for voting. The General put his Crawford ballot aside, picked up the Adams ballot, and voted for the man from Massachusetts.

Daniel Webster announced the result: 13 votes for John Quincy Adams, seven for Andrew Jackson, and four for William H. Crawford.

John Quincy Adams, by the narrowest of majorities in the House of Representatives, was the sixth President of the United States.

CHAPTER 7

President
John Quincy Adams

"MAY THE blessing of God rest upon the event of this day!"
That was the reaction, and quite an understandable one,
of John Quincy Adams on learning the news that he had
been elected President of the United States.

The news had been brought to him by Alexander Everett, the friend who had gone to Russia with Adams as a
student and aide so long ago. Everett was as much a protege
of Adams as the Massachusetts man ever had, and he was
as delighted as the new President.

A handful of others came with the same news that day
and evening. Congratulations began to pour in, first from
the people of the State Department, then from political
friends and acquaintances, then from the family.

That evening, John Quincy Adams attended the President's reception—the last reception to be given in the
White House by outgoing President Monroe. John Calhoun was there. So was Henry Clay, attentively watching
the ladies, and so was General Andrew Jackson, the man
who had polled the most popular votes and the most electoral votes in the election just past—but the man, nonetheless, who was to go down as defeated candidate because of
the specific phrasing of the American Constitution.

How did the two candidates meet—one of them, the

small, heavyset one, flushed with victory, the other, the spare, leonine figure nursing the wounds of defeat? They met very well, as the event was reported later by others. Jackson spoke first, stepping forward toward the smaller man, a lady on his right arm. He extended his left hand and apologized for doing so.

Adams, shifting his eyes, replied courteously.

The incident was over, and the two men went their separate ways. Observers noted that Adams had less than the best of it. An Englishman remarked that Adams' figure was short and thick, and that he appeared to be cunning and full of guile. But Adams was at a disadvantage, now as always in his later years. He suffered from an eye disorder which made his eyes water constantly, and he found it difficult to keep his gaze fixed on any one object because of it. The impression was that he was shifty-eyed, and it was to color the impression of his total personality and give the public an unfavorable view of this sixth President of the United States.

At first, as was indicated at the Presidential reception, Andrew Jackson took the election of this minority president calmly enough.

Not so John C. Calhoun, the new Vice-President of the United States. The morning after the election, an Adams man visited Calhoun and was bluntly told that if Henry Clay were appointed Secretary of State there would be determined opposition to the new administration from the first moment, and that all Adams could expect would be support from New England.

Calhoun had the presumption, then, to tell Adams, through this intermediary, who should be Secretary of State and who should fill other cabinet posts. Apparently he believed that Adams was weak and pliable, and could be told what to do because he was a minority President.

Adams paid no attention, except to store the warning in the back of his mind, and went his own way in forming a cabinet. He appointed Henry Clay as Secretary of State, thus arousing the antipathy of the Jackson men, who claimed that a "deal" had been made before the election in the House of Representatives. Clay had traded his influence for the job, said the Jackson forces. This was the beginning almost immediately after the election, of a determined opposition—as Calhoun had suggested—which would not end for four long years.

There is little question that John Quincy Adams had made an implicit "deal" with Clay, although Clay noted that he had made up his mind to support Adams before the deal was made. Adams had also attempted to persuade Andrew Jackson to accept the Vice-Presidency, at least during one period of the campaign. He had, in other words, "played politics" although he professed a genuine hatred for politics. It is true, he did hate party politics, but he did not understand that politics exist whether or not parties do. Parties are simply orderly groupings through which politics can be made more effective. Adams' whole career is a testimony to the existence of politics within his own sphere, where he said he would have no part of them. The hope of the Revolutionary group of Presidents for a government without organized factions could not be sustained as their era passed away. They had banded together in an undertaking that was so audacious and so all consuming that it colored their views and commanded their loyalties for the rest of their lives. They could not expect the rest of America, in succeeding generations, to see the world through their eyes. Adams, having been so dependent upon his father for political orientation and having so much filial piety, tended to see the world through the eyes of these old revolutionaries, too. John Quincy Adams was a real part of the Revolution, far more than it might be expected of a boy not yet in his teens.

The world of John Quincy Adams was changing and had changed greatly in the years he lived abroad. By the time he came home to head the Department of State—an appointment for which he was eminently fitted—the tradition that the Secretary of State succeeded to the Presidency was becoming a bit timeworn. Nevertheless Adams profited by that tradition. But during his tenure of office, it became evident that the tradition would end. In an ebullient and expanding America, it was not to be left to any American President to pick his successor.

Adams nominally became the head of the only party in America, the Democratic Republican Party. But because there was only one party, he was besieged from all sides with demands for recognition of this group and that group within the cabinet. The remains of the Federalist party wanted something. So did the DeWitt Clinton faction in New York. Andrew Jackson, offered the post of Secretary of War, declined and thus ended the Era of Good Feeling and paved the way for the open break between his partisans and those of the President.

But in truth, there were very few personal partisans of the President. There has never been a President of the United States who had a smaller group of adherents and personal friends. Because he did not believe in party, he did not even have a large number of political friends or office seekers about him.

Nothing very exciting happened in John Quincy Adams' term of office—that is, the nation was not beset by threat of war from the outside or by serious internal problems. His administration was, perhaps, most noteworthy for the emphasis it placed on *national* solutions to the country's problems rather than on *state* solutions.

John Quincy Adams was not a democrat, in the sense that he believed in the unrestricted sovereignty of the people. He was a republican with a very high regard for private property. In fact, he said, at the beginning of his term that, while the rights of the individual had been well secured politically, the rights of property had not been secured. He was concerned about measures providing for a national bankruptcy law and the continuation of a national banking system, both of which were badly needed, although not fifty men in the nation seemed to understand that need.

At this time in American history, it was becoming apparent that there could be no reconciliation of two opposed views of the Constitution. One of these views was called the "strict construction" view. Strict constructionists held that the words of the Constitution were inviolate. They believed in the omniscience of the founding fathers of the nation and insisted on a literal interpretation of the Constitution.

Another group in the nation were called the "loose constructionists." These men believed that the Constitution was established to be a living document and that it could not survive if it was not subject to the broadest interpretation. The founding fathers, for example, had never seen or heard of a steamboat when they drew the Constitution. Locomotives were unknown. When the locomotive and the steamboat were perfected, transportation in the nation was revolutionized. Since the men who drew up the Constitution knew nothing about these matters, were other men to be governed by their ignorance in considering the effects of steamship and railroad transportation on the nation?

These were not future problems but immediate problems, and they must be met directly.

John Quincy Adams met them. At the time he took office, the nation was arguing about a number of highway, lighthouse, and canal propositions. Some men took the position that the Constitution permitted some of these, but forbade the federal government from interfering in others.

Were these federal problems or state problems? Neither, said John Quincy Adams. They were *national* problems and thus they were problems for the consideration of the *national* government in Washington. He advocated the establishment of national astronomical observatories, and, indeed, of a national university.

These views aroused far greater resentment in 1825 than might be believed in the second half of the twentieth century. Thus, while it is correct to say that the period of 1824-1828 was one of the least turbulent in American history, it is not correct to say that "nothing happened."

Much happened which was ultimately to affect American relationships at home and abroad.

Since the days when Adams was Secretary of State, he had been a close and careful observer of the Latin American scene. Latin America was in ferment in those years, as Simon Bolivar led what became a multi-nation revolution which spread across South America and up into Central America. By 1822 Simon Bolivar had set the wheels in motion to create a continental confederation of Latin American states. When the Monroe Doctrine was announced, it aroused hope in various Latin American leaders that the United States might be drawn into participation in Latin American affairs—at least to the extent of helping these infant nations to build their strength and to protect themselves against resurgent Spanish power.

Led by Bolivar, the Latin American nations in 1825 called for a meeting of American states to be held in Panama. The United States was asked to attend the meeting.

The invitation brought up an important question in American foreign policy—not one that would startle the world immediately, but one that would affect the nation's attitude toward world affairs in the future, and which would also establish an emotional framework for inter-American relations. The question was whether or not the United States should participate in an international Congress which might impinge on national sovereignties and involve the United States in international problems.

At that time, the keystone of American foreign policy first enunciated by Washington, was a flat refusal to engage in foreign wars or foreign disputes or foreign entanglements. John Adams, father of the new President of the United States, had subscribed to that theory and had followed it. This position predominated in all American relationships with other countries.

Henry Clay advocated an unconditional acceptance of the invitation. Adams, the wily diplomat, was far more conservative. He demanded that the United States attend the Congress as a neutral, so there would be no chance of becoming engaged in war with Spain. He asked for more time and a specific agenda or plan for discussion.

The purpose of the invitation to the United States was to turn the Monroe Doctrine into an alliance among all the states of the Western Henmisphere. Had the plan been successful, it might have resulted in partnership rather than dislike in inter-American relations.

Adams sent to Congress the names of two commissioners he wanted to dispatch to the meeting. In Congress, the names went before the Senate where John C. Calhoun was already beginning to show opposition to Adams. Calhoun, as President of the Senate, had both power and adherents to help or hinder Adams' program.

The Senate looked long and hard at the proposal, and debated it for six weeks before accepting the commissioners, even then by only a narrow margin.

Then Adams sent a request to the House for appropriations that would make American participation in the Congress possible.

Throughout these discussions Adams was accused of trying to change American foreign policy, and, in truth, that is exactly what he was attempting to do. In the past, he had been one of the strong isolationists. Now, faced with the establishment of eight new nations in South and Central America, most of them patterned on the form of government of the United States, Adams was inclined to change his mind. Times had changed. Would American policy be flexible enough to change with them?

Adams was flexible enough. The Senate victory had been won after a hard struggle. In the House, where Adams supporters dominated, it was easier. The appropriation was passed.

It is remarkable to note what *almost* happened at Panama in the year 1825. Adams and Clay drafted instructions for the ministers which, in Clay's words, were to include the establishment of a series of "good neighborhood" treaties. As diplomatic historian Samuel Flagg Bemis put it, Adams and Clay were "a century ahead of their time."

The Clay-Adams plan for a nineteenth century good neighbor policy in Latin America did not materialize. One American representative refused to travel to Panama during the terrible summer season when yellow fever and malaria plagued that land. A messenger who carried instructions to the other delegate was shipwrecked and failed to arrive.

The Latin Americans met, noted the absence of the Norteamericanos, and after conducting some business, adjourned until fall, to meet in the more healthful climate of Mexico.

Adams now felt so strongly about the importance of the

meeting that he asked James Monroe, former President, to attend the conference. Had Monroe done so, any ill-feeling caused by the original American failure to appear would have been wiped out quickly by the presence of so eminent a North American official. Had Monroe decided to go, perhaps the conference could have been saved. But Monroe did not want to go, and would not.

The conference was never held in Mexico. Bolivar, the key figure, had lost interest in what seemed to be a hopeless prospect in view of the disinterest of the United States and the attitude of Britain which wanted to block any attempt by the United States to lead a hemispheric union of any kind.

Other Latin nations, seeing evidence of the lack of interest of the United States in their problems, would be hard to rally again to such a meeting.

In the United States the public had no interest at all in a Congress of American Nations or any other meeting that might increase American commitments to anything but continental expansion. The move was westward; and all American eyes were turned toward the Pacific.

Clay, not Adams, was the man who had the foresight to realize the future importance of Latin America to the United States, but the policy, like the Monroe Doctrine must be credited to the man who approved it, and took responsibility for it. Adams was the man who did that. Had Clay been President, there would have been more enthusiasm for cooperation with the new nations in the south, and hemispheric relations might have been better for it. But in defense of Adams, his failure to press for rapport with Latin America was at least partly prompted by immediate pressing difficulties in which he found himself as President of the United States.

During the Senate debate on the Panama Mission, Sen-

ator John Randolph of Virginia arose and made some vit-
riolic statements about both Adams and Clay. The Senator
had once been involved in bitter controversy with John
Adams, and thereafter referred to the Adams family as "the
American House of Stuart." He transferred his hatred from
father to son.

One day during the debate on confirmation of the Panama conference appointees, Randolph arose to oppose the
appointments. He attacked Adams, by accusing him of a
coalition with Clay—"the combination, unheard of until
then, of the Puritan with the blackleg." He referred to Clay
in even more scalding terms, as "this being, so brilliant, yet
so corrupt, which, like a rotten mackerel by moonlight,
shines and stinks and stinks and shines."

Those were fighting words and they provoked a fight—or
rather two fights. One was between Senator Randolph and
Secretary Clay. The other was between President Adams
and Vice-President Calhoun, for Calhoun sat in his seat,
presiding over the Senate, and winked not an eye as the Senator from Virginia inflicted on the President of the United
States the most virulent attack made in the history of the
office.

The first fight was easy to predict, given the code of honor
of the day and Henry Clay's temper. Clay challenged Ran-
dalph to a duel. Randolph was inclined to plead that he had
spoken as a U.S. Senator, but the words were too harsh for
such an explanation. He accepted the challenge and chose
a spot on the Virginia shore of the Potomac river for the
scene of the duel.

The duel was to be held in the afternoon of one fine
spring day in 1826. Randolph and Clay set out by separate
carriages. When they arrived, Randolph announced to his
friend, Senator Thomas Hart Benton, that he had intended
to refrain from firing at Clay but that now he was not so

sure because he had heard that Clay was determined to try
to kill him.

The two duelists were handed their pistols. Randolph's
discharged as he was handling it, before Clay had his gun in
hand, which lent some belief to the idea that he might be
trying to rattle Clay. They took their positions tensely.

When all was ready, one of the seconds gave a quick
count of "one, two, three," and the two men fired. Benton
said the bullets each passed so close that it was a wonder
that neither man was hit.

Clay demanded another shot, although Benton had come
out of the safety of the woods and tried to mediate.

Randolph also demanded another shot, but he did not
want it. He had determined that he would not try to kill
Clay—an important decision for Clay's safety because while
Clay was totally unfamiliar with firearms, Randolph was
an expert shot.

When the second count came Clay fired, and the bullet
passed through the tail of Randolph's coat. Randolph fired
his gun in the air, then extended his hand and advanced
toward Clay, saying "You owe me a coat, Mr. Clay."

Clay replied that he was glad the debt was no greater, and
shook the extended hand.

That was the end of one duel. Honor was satisfied in the
field, and the two men could retire to Washington without
rancor.

There was no such easy solution to the battle between
John Adams and John Calhoun. Adams wrote a letter
which was published under the pseudonym Patrick Henry,
in which he attacked Calhoun for failing to stop Randolph's
vilification of the President and his administration.

Calhoun responded with an article under the name Onslow in which he attacked the administration of Adams. So
the President and Vice-President of the United States, be-

fore a year of the administration had ended, were engaged in thinly-veiled warfare. If the public at large did not know what was occurring, at least the insiders in Washington were fully aware of the identities of Patrick Henry and Onslow.

The only positive thing to come out of the argument was a change in the rules of the U.S. Senate. Adams had argued that the Vice-President had a responsibility to keep Senators from abusing the President of the United States, and thus to protect the name and position of the Presidency. Calhoun argued that he was not a member of the Senate, but simply its presiding officer, and that thus he had no right to limit debate in any way.

Shortly afterward the Senate changed its rules to allow the Vice-President to control debate if it seemed to be getting out of hand.

Throughout much of the remainder of his administration, Adams was engaged in warfare with John Randolph. It was said that after the Panama Mission vote, he never won another battle in Congress, that each measure sponsored by the administration went down to defeat, and that administration support of a bill was like a kiss of death.

Adams' record in the White House was notable for several other reasons, however. He adopted a principle that was to be forgotten later, but was to be recognized finally as the only means of preserving good government. He refused to discharge men who served well in office even if they were politically opposed to him. Henry Clay came to him one time, insisting that a particular officer at New Orleans be fired because he was reviling Adams, Clay, and the Louisiana men who had voted for Adams in the House contest.

Adams refused to discharge the man or any other men who served in federal office, simply because of their opinions. He claimed to have discharged only two men during his entire term, and those for proven bad conduct in office.

True to his distaste for party politics, Adams refused to engage in politics at all, at least as far as parties were concerned, and thus sealed his own political doom. Thurlow Weed came to Washington to see Adams, a man who was fast becoming an important political figure in New York State. Weed wanted Adams to appoint a man from New York to represent the United States abroad in one of the important posts. The man in question was General Tallmadge, who had been instrumental in winning New York's electoral votes for Adams, and thus giving him his chance to become president.

Adams met with Weed, but he refused to heed Weed, or to do anything for Tallmadge. It was the last call Weed paid at the White House during the Adams administration. The President had firmly closed the door. He had alienated New York, too.

As President, Adams led a simple life, and was not surrounded by ceremony or the pomp and protection that we associate with Presidents today. No Secret Service men followed him. He was accustomed to arising before dawn and going down to the Potomac, quite alone, for a swim. In bitter weather he would go for a long walk in Washington, again quite alone.

Many in Washington knew of the President's habit, but no one bothered him on these morning excursions. When General Lafayette returned to the United States on his triumphal tour, Adams accompanied Lafayette to visit President James Monroe. They set out in two coaches, without escorts or fanfares, and when they, along with Monroe, visited another statesman, Adams and Monroe shared a single bedroom in the man's house one night.

This informality was possible because there was no aura of mystery about the Presidency. The President was regarded as a citizen entrusted with the responsibility for operation of the Executive Branch of the government. His term was short. He was in no sense a super-man, and particularly did the public recognize this of Adams.

Adams' willingness to cultivate enemies but not friends made it certain, before the administration was two years old, that he could not be reelected President. In the elections of 1826 the people sent back to Washington a Congress that was overwhelmingly anti-administration in both houses. Andrew Jackson, whiling away his time at the Hermitage, his house in Tennessee, was the gray figure who loomed over Adams for the next two years.

Politicking for Jackson had never ceased, from the day he set out on his slow trip to Tennessee in 1825, to be cheered by an excited populace all the way. There was no question in 1828 that Jackson was the man of the people.

But that very fact made him political enemies. The group in America who believed in government by a governing class, feared Jackson. He was not an educated man. He was a military man. He was a westerner. He was of humble birth. He was everything that no other President had been and nothing that the others had been.

In a sense, then, the entire contest that was to be waged for the election of 1828 revolved around Andrew Jackson, not around the man who occupied the White House.

CHAPTER **8**

The Victory of Andrew Jackson

SINCE THERE were so few issues that seemed to be of grave importance in these days, the victory of Adams in the election of 1824 made it certain that the election of 1828 would be a bitter contest between personalities.

But there was more to politics in the next four years than might seem apparent, for the political attitude of the people of the United States was changing rapidly. The idea that the Presidency should be held by a wise and deserving man was dying. With the growth of presidential power, which was unavoidable in the growth of the nation and the growth of government, the President dispensed more jobs and more favors. Presidents would continue to follow their own ideas but Adams was more beholden to other men than any of the previous Presidents had been. In this period, after 1824, began the forging of political parties as we know them. Parties as political instruments replaced the old flimsy blocs and cliques whose very flimsiness had made them unwieldy.

Martin Van Buren was the man who planned to put Andrew Jackson in the White House. Perhaps Jackson would have gotten there anyhow, but early in the presidential term of John Quincy Adams, Van Buren began lining up a combination of southern planters and northern businessmen to oppose Adams. These Jackson men used some very interesting tricks in Congress. They came out for a single term for the President. They came out against presidential patronage. They cried in horror when the President asked a man who had been elected to Congress to take another federal post. (This last was an open slap at the appointment of Clay as Secretary of State from his job as Speaker of the House of Representatives.)

The Jackson-Van Buren men did not really expect their criticisms to change Adams' policies. But by bringing the matters up in Congress, they drew public attention to these problems. They convinced many people that the Adams administration was hungrily seeking power in its attempts to bring "nationalism" to American affairs.

In his first message to Congress after the election, President Adams introduced several of the issues of the coming campaign. His demand for creation of a national university was to be one major issue. Another was the President's strong support of federal authority to build roads, canals, and other public structures that would benefit the people as a whole regardless of their adherence to any single state.

The friends of Andrew Jackson made their plans for 1828. Martin Van Buren and other enemies of Adams formed central committees of correspondence in each state. Under each central committee a number of local committees furnished materials to the press and public. The words "committees of correspondence" sound strange in the twentieth century. One must recall that the telegraph did not yet exist (Samuel Finley Breese Morse was to visit Andrew Jackson a few years later and plead for its support). Steamboats were as yet imperfect, and inclined to burst their boilers on little provocation. The roads about which President Adams spoke were dustmills in the summer and sinkholes in the winter. There were two important methods of communication between office-seeker and the public. One was the newspaper. The other was the small public meeting in the town square or before the village general store.

Jackson's committees of correspondence wrote articles for the newspapers. The members persuaded many editors to support the General. The committees started their own newspapers. They sponsored mass meetings and public musters of the militia. They held barbecues and fish fries. And at each of these meetings, members of the committees appeared before the crowds to make orations. Their orations were long and windy. The people liked good strong speeches in those days and from 1825 to 1828 they could not have asked for more fire and brimstone in political affairs than was delivered to them by General Jackson's adherents. The Jackson men attacked the centralization of government under Adams. They attacked Adams and Clay for striking an "iniquitous bargain" which brought Adams to the Presidency. They never stopped praising General Jackson as a man of the people, and attacking Adams as a "prince of privilege."

When the Adams administration was inaugurated in March, 1825, Andrew Jackson, still a United States senator, left Washington for his home at the Hermitage in Tennessee. He must decide within a few weeks whether to return to the United States Senate or to resign and make himself available as a full-time candidate for the Presidency in 1828. From the moment of Adams' election there was no getting away from that problem, and had Jackson been totally innocent of ambition the pressures on him were so great that he could hardly refuse them. For he became the point of focus of all the resentments and angers of the westerners. John Quincy Adams represented to them the old way of doing things, the class system, the imperiousness of the educated. Andrew Jackson, Old Hickory, was adopted as a "man of the people." This was to become the campaign cry of his adherents.

Shortly after the election of Adams and the return of Jackson to his plantation, four thousand Kentucky men attended a barbecue to honor the four Kentucky congressmen who had voted for Jackson in the election, although Kentucky's Henry Clay had thrown his support to Adams. There was no overlooking this slap at Clay from his home state. It launched the Jackson campaign. In the summer of 1826, Henry Clay came home to Kentucky, and the Secretary of State was met by his own adherents, who gave a dinner for him, but the number of Clay supporters had shrunk so alarmingly in 1826 that the governor of the state refused to attend the dinner and so did many other important state officers and newspaper editors.

It was apparent that summer that Andrew Jackson had made his decision and was seeking the Presidency openly. He perfected the theme of corruption. At Nashville, Jackson told the voters that he had not sought the nomination in the first place in 1824 and had made no attempt to influence the House of Representatives. The people cheered wildly. A few weeks after his return to Tennessee, Jackson resigned his Senate seat, for, as he told the Tennessee assemblymen, it might be improper to continue in that office, since the Assembly had just officially nominated Andrew Jackson for the Presidency as the candidate of the state of Tennessee.

All that summer Jackson continued to campaign. On the Fourth of July he was asked to make the Independence Day oration at Franklin. He told the enthusiastic crowd that the high distinction of the Presidency had vanished in this administration, because Adams had won election against the wishes of the people.

By the autumn of 1826 the Jackson campaign had shown a high degree of success. In the congressional elections majorities of anti-Adams men won control of both the House and the Senate. Adams, then, was no longer just a minority president, but a minority President who faced a hostile Congress. It was a new situation for America, and it was to bring a test of the validity of the principle of separation of powers that had been laid down by the men who drew the Constitution.

In December, 1826, Adams and Henry Clay discussed the Presidential election that was still two years off. Neither man seemed to realize that his chance again to be a candidate for the Presidency was lost—Clay's because of the charge of "bargain" and Adams' because he was the symbol of the past.

Just before Christmas in 1826 Clay told President Adams that friends had suggested that Clay run for the Vice-Presidency in 1828. Adams did not like Clay's suggestion. He said that if Clay found the office of Secretary of State too difficult then Clay ought to run for the Vice-Presidency. But as far as Adams was concerned, he hoped that Clay would stay in the State Department because he would find Clay difficult to replace as Secretary of State. It was clear that Adams would run again in 1828, and that he still believed he would win a second term.

But the new Congress of 1826 contained a number of the leaders who had opposed John Quincy Adams' election. Among them was John Randolph of Virginia. Randolph had not been returned to the Senate by the Virginia legislature largely because of his intemperate attack on Adams and the duel with Clay, but Randolph was elected when he ran for the House. And in the House, Randolph continued to lay waste to the administration program. The charge was the same: corruption and waste. The reason was more personal: John Randolph hated Adams, the father, and he transferred that hatred to Adams, the son. His feelings seemed even to grow stronger in his diatribes against what he called the "dynasty" of the Adams family.

John Quincy Adams now showed openly the contempt he had always felt for political parties. Adams refused to build a political machine by use of the power of appointment to federal jobs. Secretary Clay suggested such a policy, when the occasion arose in connection with an appointee who was openly opposed to this Administration. Clay indicated that Adams ought to reward his friends and eliminate his known enemies from federal jobs.

"To answer that it is the pleasure of the President would be harsh and odious—inconsistent with the principle upon which I have commenced this administration," Adams said. Once he began such a policy, the President added, where would it end? "An invidious and inquisitorial scrutiny into the personal dispositions of public officers will creep through the whole Union, and the most selfish and sordid passions will be kindled into activity. . ." Here Adams gave as clear a view of the dangers of the spoils system as any executive had ever shown.

Adams' attitude toward appointments did not prevent his enemies from indicating that he had turned the federal government into a huge soup pot from which he ladled sustenance for his friends. But the Jackson men were not alone in their insults; on both sides the struggle between John Quincy Adams and Andrew Jackson was notable for its lack of restraint and its casual treatment of the truth. Yet—what was truth in the matter of the power of appointment? Samuel Flagg Bemis suggests that, while earlier historians and biographers had attributed to Adams a firm stand on principle in his refusal to oust political opponents from office, Adams had believed this was good politics, too, and if he kept the old office holders they would be loyal to him. It was hard to know where truth lay, because one of the disquieting characteristics of John Quincy Adams was to say one thing to one person, another to a second, and to confide his most personal thoughts—sometimes at variance with his public statements—only to his diary.

The argument that Adams stood on principle is given strength by his refusal to appoint his friends to public office, much to the exasperation of Adams men everywhere. From South Carolina a supporter wrote to the President, complaining that the administration was ruining itself by failing to support its friends. In Philadelphia Adams appointed a number of anti-Adams men to office, including the postmaster, a Jackson man. Adams supporters all across the nation complained, but it was in Adams' character to meet complaint with stubbornness. A firm supporter suggested that the refusal of the government to reward its friends, even when those friends were highly qualified, threw them to the enemy. Adams replied by inviting that supporter to join the enemy himself.

In Pennsylvania, then, the cause was nearly lost. In New York, Adams rewarded the supporters who had made it possible for him to win election in 1824 with equal lack of tact and sensitivity. When Thurlow Weed came to call, Adams nearly ignored him, and among the half dozen men in New York who had worked hardest for Adams, none received either distinction or reward from the President of the United States.

It seemed almost to be a calculated policy of self-destruction. Friend, acquaintance, supporter—all came to Washington seeking jobs. If the jobs were for themselves they went home in disappointment. If the jobs were for others, and if the men were qualified, still the politicians fared little better. Adams seemed truly annoyed to be asked for anything. Adams was thoroughly insensitive. No matter how much he indulged himself in scourging and introspection in the privacy of his bedroom, where he sat for hours, late at night and early in the mornings, writing in his diary, he still showed no sign of understanding the legitimate hopes of others.

In New Jersey, in Ohio, in every corner of the Union, Adams men could point to some instance in which a supporter had been slighted or an enemy rewarded. It was indeed a wonder that Adams maintained any political support at all. The basis for the support he held was certainly not affection, for no President inspired less affection during his term of office than John Quincy Adams. Some of Adams' support came from the enemies of Andrew Jackson and of militarism, but a large part of it came from the strong and sturdy following of Henry Clay, who had cast his lot with the tight-lipped Adams.

As election time neared in 1828 the issues of the campaign were not much clearer than before, except the issue of personalities. One issue was the tariff. If he were to finance the internal improvements which he felt the federal government should undertake Adams must have money. The tariff, the tax on imported goods, was the acceptable means for the raising of large amounts of federal money. But the South detested the high tariff since the South bought manufactured goods and sold cotton, tobacco, and sugar. Andrew Jackson managed to take an equivocal position on the tariff, indicating (through his followers) that he favored both sides—his men took the position that appealed to any region where the tariff discussion was being held. Adams favored a high tariff, and, of course, was accused of doing so selfishly to protect the manufacturing interests of the New England states. The fact that Adams would protect no one swayed very few votes. The question

of the manner of making internal improvements was another issue, and in this one Adams took the initiative, demanding the strong federal power it would take to build
roads and canals. Again the southerners opposed him.

But issues were secondary. Personalities were the key to
the campaign, and neither man could escape vilification by
the supporters of the other.

The personal campaigning of the two candidates was
ended before the summer of 1828. Political style called for
presidential candidates to "rise above" politics, so they laid
the groundwork well in the years before their campaigns,
then let their supporters carry the burden during the last
few months. There were certain advantages to such a system. For one thing, the candidate could not be trapped into
speaking out on immediate issues, where he might have
inadequate information or less than adequate judgment.
Most important, that system was acceptable because transportation and communication were so poor that the men
must be judged on long-term characteristics and positions.

The system suited the times, but such a system also called
into play, when a need was indicated, the most ignoble of
journalistic practices. Newspapers in the first half of the
nineteenth century were unrestrained organs of opinion.
For the most part they made no pretense of "objectivity"
but showed the opinions of their editors, who reflected the
opinions of their supporters, and often of their financial
backers. From New Orleans to Boston pro-Adams newspapers attacked Jackson unmercifully, and pro-Jackson
newspapers did not spare Adams, politically or personally.

Two of the most important newspapers in America were
the *Daily National Journal,* which supported Adams, and
the *United States Telegraph,* which supported Jackson.
Adams and Clay often contributed unsigned articles to
the *Journal.* The *Telegraph* had been purchased for Editor

Duff Green with the money of Jackson supporters. The *Daily National Journal* was favored by the administration with its legal advertising of the federal laws. The *United States Telegraph* was favored by the anti-Adams House and Senate with their legal advertising. So the two forces were well-matched.

The *Journal* attacked Jackson in the most cutting manner possible—through his wife, Rachel, who had been married before she met the General. Her first husband was a man named Lewis Robards, a well-to-do Kentucky planter, whom Rachel Donelson had married before she was eighteen. Robards was a jealous man. He soon suspected Rachel of dalliance with a boarder in the house, and sent her home to her family. When Rachel went home, she met Andrew Jackson, then a young lawyer. Robards came back to the Donelson house in the Cumberland district and made up with his wife. But soon he deserted her again, and she "eloped" with Andrew Jackson.

Apparently Jackson had acted as the agent of Rachel's family, in taking her away from the Robards house. But Robards insisted that Jackson had made love to his wife and had taken her away from him. Eventually in 1790 Rachel was divorced by Lewis Robards and married Jackson, at least she and Jackson thought that a divorce had been granted. In fact it had not, because what they thought was a divorce was an enabling act granted by the Virginia legislature just before Kentucky split off from Virginia to become a state. In the cloudy legal world of the back country Jackson married Mrs. Robards before she was legally divorced from Robards, and Robards waited two full years before charging Jackson and his wife with adultery. So Jackson and Rachel were married again in 1794.

The strange story was dredged up to try to injure Jackson politically in 1824, but in 1828 it became an important part of the political campaign. Thomas Arnold, a candidate for Congress in Tennessee, issued a slanderous pamphlet about Jackson and his marriage. Arnold accused Jackson of having spent his life in cock-fighting, horse-racing, dueling, and of stealing Rachel Robards, first having "driven Robards off like a dog and taken his wife." The implication was not that Jackson had been involved in a complicated affair of the heart, but that the General had seen a woman he wanted, and had taken her away from her husband.

Undoubtedly the *Journal* knew the story was ridiculous and false when it was printed. But that did not stop the newspaper from repeating it. President Adams did not lift a finger to stop the publication. Once the story was published he did not lift a finger to deny it or secure a retraction.

So the campaign sank into the mud. The pro-Jackson *Telegraph* attacked the President and his Secretary of State, week in and week out. Editor Duff Green said that Adams was a monarchist, and that he intended to establish an "aristocratical and hereditary government" in the United States. Those words came from a scurrilous pamphlet, but they were picked up with gusto by the *Telegraph*. The newspaper suggested that Clay had been bribed to throw his vote to Adams in 1824. Green indicated that the administration was made up of corrupt gangsters who were robbing the public purse. In a painstaking analysis of Adams' career, his enemies discovered that he had been paid an average of $12,500 a year by the federal government during his career in public office. Adams, said the enemy, lived only to root in the public trough.

Not to be outdone, the anti-Adams men circulated rumors about the marital affairs of the Adamses.

No insult was too vile to be heaped on the opposition candidate by the supporters of both sides. No rumor could be neglected; no misstatement about the enemy could be or would be corrected. For enemy was the proper word; Jackson and Adams did not speak to one another again after the election of 1824, and the inauguration ball at which Jackson had comported himself so elegantly.

Andrew Jackson and Adams both did some quiet electioneering in the campaign. Adams used the Fourth of July to make a political speech about his internal improvement program. Jackson used the 13th anniversary of his New Orleans victory to travel to that southern city, to be lionized, and to win votes. He and Mrs. Jackson and a party of politicians and war veterans boarded the steamboat *Pocahontas* and sailed down the Mississippi. James Alexander Hamilton of New York was in the party, a presence that was significant, because the election would hinge on the vote in New York and Pennsylvania. In Pennsylvania, Adams had done great harm to himself, and James Buchanan worked steadily for the election of Jackson.

Andrew Jackson, a slave owner, would capture all the southern states without question. Adams *must* carry New England and the Atlantic states, and the west. It was not at all certain that he would carry the western states north of the Ohio river, so Pennsylvania and New York loomed all the more important. Jackson would surely carry all the western states south of the Ohio, for he was a westerner himself.

By autumn the issues of the campaign had melted down to one: it was Jackson and the common people against Adams and the elite. Or so it was with Jackson's people in Jackson territory, but even in the south and west Jackson had enemies, and bitter ones. One of the most vicious campaign documents of all was a flyer which portrayed the coffins of men killed by Jackson—murdered by him, said his enemies. And after the election, so great was the feeling to remain that a schoolboy, when asked who had slain the Biblical Abel, replied that Andrew Jackson was the villain.

The feelings of John Quincy Adams during this campaign are masked, for he abandoned his diary between August 6 and December 1, 1828. But before that time Adams gave vent to his feelings on the subject.

He told of one meeting of a Jackson group in Baltimore, a meeting he observed on his summer trip north. The meeting was held in the square next to Barnum's House. A young man named McMahon, a member of the state legislature, spoke to the crowd for nearly three hours about the sins of the administration and the virtues of Andrew Jackson. Inside Barnum's, President John Quincy Adams met a steady stream of well-wishers who wanted to shake the President's hand.

Adams was in bed before eleven, when the indefatigable Mr. McMahon stopped speaking. The President noted for his diary's sake that such meetings were held every day of the week. "A stranger would think that the people of the United States have no other occupation than electioneering," he said.

Perhaps it was apparent to Adams in August that he was a defeated man. His last pre-election diary comment came on August 6, when he told of arriving in Philadelphia to be followed along the wharf by a cheering crowd. But he did not fail to note that in the milling he heard cries of "Huzza for Jackson." That was his last word in the diary until December.

The election for the Presidency was held not on one day in every state but according to the laws of the various states, and voting took place between the last day of October and

November 5. The presidential candidate and the vice-presidential candidate of the party that called itself National Republican were John Quincy Adams and Richard Rush. They were defeated by Andrew Jackson and John C. Calhoun, who polled 647,000 of the 1,150,000 votes cast. The electoral vote was 178 votes for Jackson and 83 for Adams.

☆ ☆ ☆

CHAPTER 9

Congressman Adams

JOHN QUINCY ADAMS was convinced that he had been defeated by narrow sectionalism, and he remained so convinced a decade later. He had never advocated a high tariff for its own sake—although he had signed the monstrous and irresponsible Tariff of Abominations bill which was offered in 1827. In his own defeat, Adams saw the end to the movement he sponsored to direct national energies to the improvement of the whole country, without regard for the peculiar interests of states and regions. He did not understand in 1828 or at any time later that the nature of the United States had undergone a basic change with the opening of the West.

The reaction of John Quincy Adams to his defeat was a combination of disappointment, self-pity, and hurt. At first he believed that his political life was ended. But as a steady stream of visitors continued to call at the White House in the winter of 1828-29, Adams' spirits rose a little. It was hard to tear himself away from the routine of the White House, for he had lived there four long years. Like many of his contemporaries, Adams maintained many interests. He was a fine horticulturist, and had planted in the White House grounds Spanish cork oaks, black walnut trees, almond trees, ash and ash-leaved maples, lilacs, and other trees and bushes. During his years in the White House, Adams had maintained the long routine to which he had accustomed himself from his earliest years. He arose before daylight, winter and summer, wrote for two or three hours and then went horseback riding. Sometimes his day began at five in the morning, sometimes before four o'clock. He alternated his rides with swimming in the Potomac, and sometimes he combined a ride of twelve miles or so and a swim at the end of it before returning to the White House and the cares of the day.

All this was to pass after March 4. Adams could not return to Massachusetts that early in the year. His wife's health would not permit it, since the trip would expose her to uncertain weather and many hardships. So he decided to rent the house of Commodore David Porter in the country, about a mile and a half from the White House. As March 4 drew near, Adams began to remove his belongings to this house called Meridian Hill.

A certain amount of contact between Adams and the incoming President Jackson was necessary, but it was carried out through intermediaries. Jackson was angry with all who had slandered his wife, and understandably so. Although he had won the election in spite of the evil campaign, his wife had died, and Jackson was never to give up his belief that the slanderers had killed her. Chief among them he placed John Quincy Adams, for he was certain that had Adams wanted the campaign stopped it would have been stopped. Adams denied all responsibility.

There was another reason that the two would not meet again, a reason unknown to the public and to most politicians. Adams was a long-hating man and he had been deeply stung by the charges made against him and his administration by the Jackson supporters. They had gone so far during the campaign as to attack Adams for purchasing a billiard table with his own money, and they charged that Adams was turning the White House into a gambling den.

This calumny and others convinced Adams that General Jackson was not a gentleman.

Jackson came to Washington in February and took residence at Gadsby's Tavern, where hundreds of politicians, well-wishers, and favor seekers visited him. Washington was yet a small town, but twenty thousand people massed at the Capitol and along the streets to see Jackson take the oath of office. On the day before, John Quincy Adams concluded his duties as President of the United States. He dealt with several minor measures and journeyed to the Capitol at noon to deliver messages to both houses, regarding the affairs of the nation. He signed fifteen bills passed by this Twentieth Congress, and informed a joint committee of the houses that he had no further communication except to wish every member health and happiness in the future. He walked back to the White House convinced that his public life was over and consulted with his cabinet members as to whether or not he should attend the inauguration. All except Richard Rush opposed the idea, so he decided to follow his own inclination and stay away.

The next day, March 4, Andrew Jackson was inaugurated. To understand what happened that day, one must recall Daniel Webster's words—for Webster was a witness to the events of the week of March 4, 1829. "I never saw anything like it before," Webster said. "They really seem to think the country is rescued from some dreadful danger." The Massachusetts man was referring to the crowds of buckskinned backwoodsmen and greasy mule skinners who roamed the streets of Washington, sleeping a half dozen men to a bed, charging into taverns and stumbling out of them. Biographer James Parton, a fastidious man, noted in writing of the event later that "it was like the inundation of northern barbarians into Rome."

There was more to the Jacksonian triumph than that

statement would make it appear. Martin Van Buren and the lesser wizards of the Jackson group had welded together around the heroic figure of Andrew Jackson a new political movement—the Democratic party. The party was a combination of the growing city political machines in the North (an emerging Tammany Hall for one) and the planters of the South with the rude but vigorous republicans of the West. Van Buren had made the combination, but Andrew Jackson was to take control of it as President and make of the Democratic party the instrument of his will during the next eight years. The dreams of two Adamses, Washington, and Hamilton of a strong national concentration of power in the hands of an elite group of leaders was blasted, not to rise again in the nineteenth century.

The Inauguration ceremony over, General Jackson rode to the White House on horseback, with a shouting, amiable mob at his heels. Washington society, aristocrats for the most part, shuddered behind their handkerchiefs and fans and top hats. Chief Justice John Marshall, an undistinguished looking man, refrained from showing his revulsion, as he had when he gave Jackson the oath of office. But all these conservatives who had maintained control of the government of the United States since its formation, with a mild exception in the Jeffersonian period, were aghast at the familiarity with which Jackson's followers treated him. Jackson surprised them and shocked them with his easy acceptance of this familiarity. These easterners did not understand the code under which Jackson and the westerners lived, under which easy manners or breeziness were not signs of disrespect or over familiarity. They did not know that Jackson would keep himself in his place of command and his subordinates in their places by methods far more important than the exercise of protocol. Some of them suspected as much, however, when Jackson refused the pomp of a military parade. His appearance at the Capitol, without fanfare, was so distinguished that a handful of wealthy observers began to suspect that they were witnessing a basic change in American governmental affairs which might not be altogether for the worse. But the Adams philosophy could never accept such a change.

When Jackson arrived at the White House, John Quincy Adams was not there to witness the public reception of the new President. The mob milled through the mansion Adams had just vacated. Rough backwoodsmen in hobnailed boots stood atop the polished tables for a better view of Old Hickory. Old soldiers and seamy-faced Indian scouts spilled whiskey and chicken on the expensive rugs, and ground the debris into the fabrics. Clothing was torn, glasses and china were broken carelessly in the crush. Congressmen and their wives had to force their way into the White House through the noisy mob. Jackson was nearly overwhelmed, and his friends managed to extricate him from the dangerous attentions of his followers only by forming a human cordon around him, and physically restraining well-wishers while the President escaped out the back entrance to the White House and made his way to the safety of Gadsby's. The mob which had overrun the executive mansion grew drunker and more disorderly, but finally began to disintegrate in its own excesses. "A regular Saturnalia," one legislator called the reception in describing it to Martin Van Buren, who was detained in New York that day. The mob was drawn outside the house, finally, when some embryo general conceived the idea of placing tubs of punch on the White House lawn, and locking the doors behind the departing guests.

That same day the now slim and almost wizened Adams rode into Washington with an attendant, keeping clear of the White House, then turning back along F street and over College Hill to the rented house. He knew nothing of the raucousness at the mansion he had occupied until a day before. He was concerned that he, John Quincy Adams, be preserved from the vices of indolence and despondency and indiscretion.

The bitterness with which this strong old figure accepted the manner of his defeat was not lessened by the events of the next few days. Antoine, the butler who had served him since 1814, had chosen to remain in the White House, in the service of Adams' enemy. Henry Clay came to Meridian Hill to pay his respects on March 12, just before Clay returned to Kentucky to rebuild his own political fortunes. But Clay did not treat Adams as the head of the political movement to which he belonged. He came to pay a courtesy call only, and remarked on leaving that he would like to hear occasionally from the former President. Adams was correct in one reading he had taken of his own situation. As the defeated President, he was not regarded as titular leader of his political movement.

That was understandable since Adams had constantly denied the legitimacy of the existence of any political movement other than one of national unity, with himself and his friends at the head of it. In effect no political movement existed at this moment except the Democratic party. The Adams concept of government was dead, and the movement that would be called Whig was in the processes of birth. Henry Clay would run for the Presidency in 1832 on the ticket of the National Republican party, but two years later he and John C. Calhoun would combine forces in the Whig movement.

During the six weeks that followed the Jackson inauguration, John Quincy Adams settled into a routine at Meridian Hill. His major concern was to answer a demand by a number of Federalist leaders of Massachusetts that he present proof of his charges that the *Essex Junto* had in fact existed and had planned to set up a northern confederacy that would withdraw from the Union and establish an alliance with Great Britain. Adams called the group the Thirteen Confederates. He worked hard on his answer; before he was finished he was to write two of them, and one was to run to more than 80,000 words. In his answer he made harsh judgments about the policies of Thomas Jefferson and Alexander Hamilton. Adams' intent was to use the answer as a statement of his own beliefs in strong national government. He was wise enough, however, to show his writings to acquaintances and supporters, and they persuaded him to withhold from publication the second and stronger statement.

In May Adams learned of the apparent suicide of his eldest son, George Washington Adams, who had fallen or jumped from a steamship en route to join his father in Washington. The younger Adams had made so sorry a tangle of his life that his brother noted the death was "not untimely", but Adams and his wife were plunged in grief at the news. On that note he traveled home to Massachusetts to take up residence. His wife felt so unwell that she decided to stay in Washington until the clamor of homecoming had ended in Quincy.

Most of the remainder of the year 1829 was spent in putting his personal affairs in the best order he could manage. At home in Quincy he found it necessary to refurnish the mansion he had inherited from his father. He considered abandonment of the house and the building of another, but found that he could not afford to do so. He could not even afford to build an adequate library in the big house for his collection of books—the finest owned by any man in America. He faced other troubles, including severe losses in an abortive venture in grist and flour milling in Washington.

In Quincy the Adams family was greeted warmly by neighbors and friends of long standing. In Boston the greeting was much less pleasant, for the political enmities he had aroused in his attacks on the *Essex Junto* and the old order of Boston politics did not endear him to the friends of his youth.

Adams faced one problem on the heels of another. He was worth $100,000 when he left the Presidency, but many of his assets were tenuous, and he found it difficult to maintain them. Financial worries, coupled with his own restlessness, weighed heavily on him, but he retained his serenity and strength by continuing his personal habits of hard work. He watched Andrew Jackson pursue the opposite of the Adams civil service policy, turning the federal government machinery into a political spoils bin from which Jackson rewarded the men who helped him. He wrote on this and other affairs in his journals. He spent many hours in the gardens of the Quincy mansion, digging up the soil, planting where trees and shrubs had died out in the years of near-abandonment. He set to work to write a biography of his father. When the water was warmed up that summer, he went swimming with his nephews several times a week, at Daniel Greenleaf's wharf, where Black's Creek emptied into Quincy Bay. He counted his strokes: 238 strokes downstream and 293 against the current to return. It was a half mile in all, and he was sixty-two years old.

In December John Quincy Adams rejoined Louisa and his son John and family in Washington. The Meridian Hill house had been sold by Commodore Porter, and Louisa and the younger Adams family had moved to a house on Sixteenth Street. Adams pursued his literary efforts and his studies there, and he met occasionally with political leaders, but never with the man who had displaced him in the White House. The next year—1830—Adams brought Louisa home to Quincy for the summer, and was pleased

to find that the attitude of his Boston friends had undergone some change since the previous year.

In 1829, when Adams had returned to Massachusetts,
there had been several shocks. The American Academy of
Arts and Sciences had dropped him as president, although
he had held that office during his absenteeism in Washington as Secretary of State and President. The Athenaeum
attempted to cancel his membership, although he was a
charter member of the organization. The new mayor of
Boston, one of the Thirteen Confederates to whom Adams
had addressed himself, gave the former President only a
slighting invitation to the important Independence Day
celebration at Faneuil hall. But in 1830, Boston began to
thaw. Harvard University elected him to the Board of Overseers. He was invited to take part in the celebration honoring the two hundred years of settlement of Boston. Most
important, he was nominated that year and elected to represent the Plymouth district as United States Representative
in the Twenty-second Congress. Having served as Ambassador, Senator, Secretary of State and President of the
United States, Congressman John Quincy Adams was to
begin a new career at the age of sixty-three. He had been a
minority President, but in the election to Congress he received three quarters of all the votes cast.

Adams' son, Charles Francis Adams, and others in the
family thought it was beneath the dignity of a former President to serve in the lower house, but John Quincy Adams
thought otherwise. Also, he welcomed the income he would
receive as a congressman (eight dollars a day while Congress was in session, plus a travel allowance). Like several of
the other former Presidents, Adams found himself badly
embarrassed financially. He owed more than $40,000 and
his assets were largely held in land, which was not easily
parted with or sold. On his way to Washington that winter,

result was to bring the tariff issue and the rights of
states and federal government in lawmaking to a crisis.
A tariff law, placing taxes on goods brought in from
abroad, helps the native industries which make those same
goods because it raises the price of foreign goods and gives
the native industries a competitive advantage. As an agri-
cultural state which grew tobacco and cotton, but paid
hard cash for shoes and kettles, South Carolina detested
high tariffs on manufactured goods. In 1830, when John
Quincy Adams was elected to the House from Massachusetts, the voters of South Carolina returned a majority of
legislators who believed in the right of the state government
to nullify the federal tariff by passing a state law against it.
They felt secure in their position, because President Andrew Jackson had held earlier that the state of Georgia had
the right to regulate Indian lands within the boundaries
of the state, no matter what arrangements had been made
by treaty between the Indians and the federal government
of the United States. The South Carolinians took the position that Jackson had already upheld the doctrine of Nullification—the primary importance of state laws over federal
laws. They were ready to advance, by calling a constitutional convention in South Carolina to nullify the tariff of
1828 as far as it concerned South Carolina. That year, however, the Nullifiers could not raise the two-thirds majority
necessary to achieve their end. So they waited, and passed
indicative if forceless resolutions against the tariff.

In the summer of 1831, before the Twenty-second Congress convened, John Quincy Adams was asked to make the
Fourth of July address at Quincy town's meeting house. He
devoted his address to reexamination of the intent of the
founding fathers in drawing the Constitution, and affirmed
the principle that no state or combination of states could
nullify any federal law except through the established man-

Adams stopped off in New Yo
President, James Monroe, and wa.
Monroe's financial situation was e
America had little sympathy for its
executives.

The Twenty-second Congress did
year later, a year that John Quincy
usual method of study and contempla
difference, however. For the first time, l
willing to make up differences with an old
was not Jackson—this was never to be. It v
houn with whom Adams had parted compai
was to be social, not political, but the returi
amenities marked a change, and a positive on
had been nearly as strong in his feelings agains
opposed him as Jackson was always to be. Latei
friendliness with Calhoun was to be marked by ai
difference in political opinion. Calhoun, displace
position as heir-apparent to the Presidency under j
was to take up the cause of states' rights as para.
over the national interest. Adams, true to his old p
ophy, was to take leadership in the struggle, brought ai
by the tariff, which led to the political debate on the is
known as Nullification. The debate centered around t.
action of one state in declaring that it would not obey
federal law. The issue was whether or not the Union would
endure, and it was here that Adams and his enemy Jackson
joined forces against Adams's friendly enemy, Calhoun.

The question of Nullification was brought to a head by
the legislators of South Carolina, after passage of the Tariff
of Abominations of 1828—the bill President Adams had
signed into law. The immediate design of the anti-Adams
congressmen and senators who had drawn the tariff law had
been to embarrass Adams in the election of 1828. The long

ner of amending the Constitution of the United States.
His father, John Adams, had given a toast on the day of his
death, another Independence Day.

"Independence forever," the old man had said in 1826.

Five years later, his aging son revised old John Adams'
words in expressing his own sentiments about the course
of the government he had seen established and had served
so many years.

"Independence and Union Forever," said John Quincy
Adams, closing his Independence Day oration.

In Massachusetts, where nullification had once begun to
flower from seeds of its own, the younger Adams' words
were greeted with cheers and respect. Copies of his address
were printed and sent to important citizens all around the
nation. Adams himself sent a copy to John C. Calhoun with
his respects. In return he received a copy of Calhoun's deci-
sive statement on the same subject. On July 26, Calhoun
had written from his South Carolina plantation at Fort Hill
on "The Relation which the States and the General Government Bear to Each Other." Herein, under his own name,
he brought forth the Doctrine of Nullification and announced his championship of it.

In essence, Calhoun said that the tariff of 1828 was a pro-
tective tariff, not a revenue tariff, and was thus unconstitutional. If the state constitutional convention of any state
would hold that any act of Congress was unconstitutional,
the law was void until three fourths of the states should
amend the Constitution, specifically to provide for the matters contained in the Congressional law. In the meantime,
any and every state had the right to nullify or outlaw the
federal law within its own state territory.

If two-thirds of the members of a South Carolina convention should decide that the Tariff of 1828 was unconstitutional, they could outlaw the tariff in South Carolina,

and it could not be enforced until it or its enabling provisions became a part of the federal constitution, passed by three fourths of the states.

Here was nullification in its artful simplicity. The blind advocates of states' rights argued that only through such policy could the Constitution and particularly Amendment Number Ten of the Bill of Rights be maintained.

The purpose of the South Carolinians, of course, was to protect their economic system, which included slavery, from dictation by a North and West that had no use for slavery and whose way of life was entirely different. Had the Doctrine of Nullification been accepted by Congress and the Administration, the Union would surely have foundered long before the Civil War, for the federal government would have been powerless to enforce national laws against any state where the laws were unpopular enough to provoke constitutional convention action; and in no arguments between regions could a three quarters ratification of an amendment have been expected, even if the federal government could have survived the long periods of time involved.

The issue was whether the Constitution of the United States represented a voluntary association of the states *temporarily* or *permanently*. Calhoun held that even if a three-fourths majority of the states decided to uphold a law that offended one state, that state still need not comply. It could then secede from the Union.

To be decided in the months that followed the statements of Adams and Calhoun was a basic question of the policies of the American federal government, the American states, and the American nation as an entity. In 1787 when the American Constitution was drawn, there was no American nation. Forty-four years later ten states which were not party to the original agreement had entered the

Union. An American nation, over and above the compact between the states, had come into being with the admission of the first new state. Whether or not this national allegiance was to grow or to shrink was the issue. It was partly because of his espousal of this superiority of nationhood over statehood that Adams had been defeated in 1828. The issue was not presented thus to the people, but it had aroused enough enemies of John Quincy Adams who found other issues to give the people; Adams' unfortunate public personality and the hero worship of the conquering general had done the rest. Now John Quincy Adams was to go back into the fight, this time as a legislator.

In 1830 Adams sincerely believed that the salvation of the Union could not be furthered by Andrew Jackson. Calhoun was Vice-President, and as far as Adams knew, Jackson was in league with the nullifiers. By 1831 Calhoun and Jackson had broken relations, after Jackson learned that Calhoun had favored punishing the General for his actions in the Seminole war and that Adams had been his protector. This breach did not convince Adams that Jackson favored union above state sovereignty, and he remained convinced that if the Union was to be saved, Congress would have to save it.

In the selection of committees for the Twenty-second Congress John Quincy Adams was thrown into a vital position when he was appointed chairman of the House Committee on Manufactures. The appointment by Speaker Andrew Stevenson meant that Adams would be the key figure in consideration of the tariff, and the tariff was the key to the move of South Carolina for nullification.

Now came a strange juxtaposition of views. Adams favored compromise to keep the nullifiers from breaking bounds. President Jackson let it be known that he would enforce the Constitution with the weapons at his disposal as chief executive. Adams did not approve of such a violent stand. He did not even take the pains to try to understand it, or to think over a toast made by Jackson at a dinner honoring the birthday of Thomas Jefferson. Jackson had then said unflinchingly: "Our Union; it must be preserved."

Adams' part in that preservation was to lead the Committee on Manufactures in the drafting of a tariff law that was to be known as the Adams Tariff of 1832. It made concessions to the South, principally by reducing the tax on the rough cloth used to clothe slaves. The law was generally regarded as an improvement over the Tariff of Abominations of 1828—but not by South Carolina.

After the new tariff law passed, Governor James Hamilton, Jr., called an extraordinary session of the South Carolina legislature. The legislature, dominated by nullifiers, called a convention, which was overwhelmingly so dominated. By a vote of 136 to 26 the convention adopted a state law nullifying the tariffs of 1828 and 1832. The legislature then passed laws for the enforcement of the state law, including provisions designed to raise a military force and appropriate money for arms.

Andrew Jackson's answer was to alert the forts in Charleston Harbor and to direct troop movements toward South Carolina. He issued a conciliatory message to Congress on December 4, 1832, and suggested further cuts in the tariff, but six days later he also issued his proclamation to the people of South Carolina, telling them that they could not nullify a federal law, nor could they leave the Union. "Disunion by armed force is treason," Jackson said.

John Quincy Adams simply did not believe what he read when he saw the report of the proclamation. He asked the House to call on Jackson for a text of the proclamation, intending to show that it conflicted with Jackson's mes-

sage to Congress. But Jackson forestalled him by voluntarily .
presenting a text, along with documents from South Carolina.

South Carolina responded to Jackson with a series of
strong resolutions, calling on other states to assemble in
general convention to consider relations between state and
federal government. The states did not respond as South
Carolina had hoped. Jackson called on Congress for a law
which would allow him to enforce revenue measures by
use of military force if necessary. The result was the Force
Bill, in which Daniel Webster led the argument against
Calhoun, now a senator, and for the Union against states'
rights.

In December when the House went into the second session, Adams was bypassed in the consideration of a new
tariff measure. The President's call for a bill was referred
to Congressman Verplanck, chairman of the Committee on
Ways and Means. In the debate the followed, Congressman
Clayton of Georgia unwisely referred to the slaves of the
South as "our machinery."

"That 'machinery,' " Adams said in a speech, "sometimes
exerts self-moving power." He declared that the people of
Massachusetts had as much right to refuse to protect the
interests of the southerners as the southerners had to refuse
to protect the rights of the North. The statement was far
more provocative than it might appear, for just two years
before, in Southampton County, Virginia Nat Turner's
slave rebellion had caused the murder of fifty-one white
people, including eighteen women and twenty-four children. Only the intervention of United States marines from
Norfolk had prevented the rebellion from spreading into
North Carolina, and perhaps through the South. Southern
planters were first terrified, then began to crack down on
their slaves with an iron hand. Adams' remark could be

and was construed to mean that Massachusetts had as much
right to refuse to send marines to put down such rebellion
as South Carolina had to nullify a tariff.

The southerners in Congress arose in a body, and charged
that Adams had thrown a firebrand into Congress. Indeed,
he had.

He went on to vote for the Force Bill. South Carolina
backed down in a way and repealed the Nullification Act.
But the convention also nullified the Force Bill, which left
a new kind of legal impasse if not an actual one. Adams,
quite stubbornly, refused to give Jackson credit for his
policies, and held that South Carolina had triumphed
through the President's delays.

Adams now became involved in many other issues, not
the least of them the Anti-Masonic movement, which was
brought to fever pitch by the murder of a fallen Mason
who threatened to reveal the secrets of the quasi-religious
order. Adams *was* opposed to the Masonic movement, but
more, he saw it as a possible means through which he might
be elected President. In 1833 he ran for governor of Massachusetts on the Anti-Masonic ticket, but was defeated.

John Quincy Adams was the victim of changing times.
He had grown to maturity in a land where partisan politics
was regarded by many leaders as wasteful and immoral.
Partisan politics existed all this while, but not in the form
of political parties as we of another century know them.
He would run for office on the ticket of the Anti-Masons,
but as he did in Congress, Adams would never acknowledge
strict allegiance to any political party. He always believed
himself to be a man of all the people. It was his misfortune
that the people did not ever share his view.

CHAPTER 10

John Quincy Adams and America

FOLLOWING defeat for the governorship of Massachusetts, John Quincy Adams returned to Congress, elected for the third time by his constituents in Plymouth district. It was a notable defeat for it revealed that Adams was not particularly well liked even in Massachusetts. His victory in the Plymouth district was significant, too, for it showed that where John Quincy Adams was known personally to the voters, he was respected and popular. This was ever to be one of Adams' problems; the bright and if not lovable, at least respected, private personality of the man contrasted severely with the dull public appearance.

The conflicts in the personality of John Quincy Adams were harsh. He was a harsh, strong man. Always he protected the things he loved, and always he fought against the people he hated. When President Andrew Jackson came to Boston on a tour in 1833, Old Hickory so impressed the leaders of the community that President Josiah Quincy of Harvard called a special meeting of the board of overseers, and the board voted to grant an honorary degree of Doctor of Laws to the President of the United States. The sole dissenting member of the board was John Quincy Adams.

Adams asked if there was not some way Harvard could avoid giving this honor.

"As the people have twice decided that this man knows enough law to be their ruler, it is not for Harvard College to maintain that they are mistaken," said President Quincy of Harvard.

Still, John Quincy Adams stayed at home on the day the degree was granted. "I would not be present to see my darling Harvard disgrace herself by conferring a Doctor's degree upon a barbarian and savage who could scarcely spell his own name," said the former President of the United States of his successor.

Adams' hopes that he might be reelected to the Presidency waned after the election of 1832, in which Henry Clay was the candidate of the men who had earlier supported Adams. The hopes ended in the election of 1836, when Daniel Webster was one of four Whig candidates who ran unsuccessfully against Martin Van Buren, Andrew Jackson's hand-picked successor. Adams and Webster disliked one another heartily, and had come into open conflict in a dispute about the foreign policy of the United States toward France. In a ringing speech on the floor of the House, Adams had replied to an earlier attack on the House by Webster in the Senate. In that speech Adams earned the title Old Man Eloquent, and the ardent dislike of Webster.

In 1836 and thereafter Adams achieved a distinction which meant much to him. He was chosen for the House that year and every two years for the rest of his life without reference to political affiliation. The people of Plymouth district selected him because he was their most distinguished citizen. Indeed, he might have been termed the most distinguished member of the House of Representatives.

As the years flew on, John Quincy Adams proved how

valuable to the nation could be a strong character in the House of Representatives who had none of the usual fears for his chances of re-election and no hesitation about pursuing the course his conscience dictated. One of his famous struggles in the House came over a resolution which was to be known in history as the Gag Rule. The argument occurred in 1836.

At that time it was apparent to John Quincy Adams that the danger of civil war in America was growing greater every year, and that slavery must be abolished in America. He was not ready to make such flat statements, but he did want as much discussion of the issues as could be brought about without actually inflaming the southern members of Congress. It was easy to inflame those southerners in 1836, for they were growing ever more sensitive to criticism and ever more fearful that the noisy Abolitionists would triumph in the North.

To control the huge mass of petitions relative to slavery that came to Congress, three resolutions were offered in May, 1836. One stated that Congress had no constitutional power to interfere with slavery in the states. The second said that Congress ought not to interfere with slavery in the District of Columbia, which was governed by Congress. The third resolution proposed that all propositions relating to slavery, which came before Congress in the future, should be laid on the table and no action taken. In other words, they should never even be discussed.

When these matters came before the House on May 18, Adams wanted to object to the last of them, particularly. After several southern members of the House had spoken in favor of the resolutions, Adams rose to attract the attention of the Speaker of the House, who could grant him the power to speak. The Speaker ignored Adams and recognized a representative from Georgia who moved to shut off debate. The House voted immediately to shut off debate before *any* objections to the resolutions had been heard.

"Am I gagged or am I not?" shouted John Quincy Adams.

He was gagged, but not for long. Adams could not speak on the issue of the resolutions, but he found another issue before the House which he could turn to his own use. Before voting on the last two resolutions, the House considered what seemed to be a harmless issue: It was a resolution which would permit the President to grant relief to the refugees from wars against the Indians. It did not seem that Adams could make any trouble over that, so he was allowed to speak.

John Quincy Adams arose and turned the discussion to talk about the general war powers of the Congress. He suggested that there might even be a civil war. Then, said Adams, "From the instant that your slaveholding states become the theater of war, civil, servile, or foreign, from that instant the war powers of Congress extend to interference with the institution of slavery in every way by which it can be interfered with . . ."

Adams was on record. He tried to go on record again when the House voted on the three resolutions about slavery. He declared on the floor of the House that the third resolution was a violation of the Constitution, and demanded that his statement be recorded in the Journal. It was not. The resolution also passed by a large vote. The Gag Rule had come into effect, and its name had come from John Quincy Adams who fought valiantly against it.

The next year Adams managed to read a petition calling for abolition of slavery in the District of Columbia on the floor of the House, despite many interruptions, but the Gag Rule was again invoked. Citizens could call on Congress to abolish slavery, but Congress would not consider anything the citizens had to say on the subject. That was the net result.

In Congress, John Quincy Adams fought the Gag Rule with all his might. He indicated that he wanted to introduce a resolution on slavery that came from slaves—or so it seemed. The southerners were up in arms in a moment, objecting. Only after they had begun to call for the censure of Adams by the House did they learn that the resolution from the "slaves" was actually an objection to abolition of slavery. They had been hoaxed!

Southerners began to refer to Adams as "The Madman of Massachusetts." A resolution was offered, calling for his censure, but it failed. Only three northerners voted for it. Adams was pleased at this vote of confidence. He was enjoying himself, and although he was in his seventies and his health was failing, he loved the fight. He loved it even when he began to receive threats against his life from southerners.

In 1838 he opposed the annexation of Texas, then a republic which sought admission to the Union. That same year, angry southerners tried to defeat him for reelection in Massachusetts by a trick. No one was nominated to oppose him in Plymouth district, but the Democrats, aligned with the South, ran a write-in campaign in favor of a well-known abolitionist. It nearly—but not quite—succeeded. Adams won again.

In the Twenty-fifth Congress, Adams proposed that the question of abolition be put up to the states as a constitutional amendment. He received masses of letters threatening his life during this period, and he felt it was necessary to explain his position. He did not favor abolition of slavery in the District of Columbia at that time, he said. He did favor the freedom of discussion of the issue. Abolition should come through constitutional means, by a constitutional amendment.

This attitude angered both the Abolitionists and the South. Adams continued to be known as the Madman of Massachusetts in the South, and he was an irritant, an unwelcome conscience, to the radicals of the North. Thoughtful Abolitionists changed their minds, however, in 1841 when John Quincy Adams took on a celebrated case that involved slavery and the slave trade, and argued it before the United States Supreme Court.

The case was that of the *Amistad,* a slave ship which had been captured by an American brig off the coast of Long Island. More than fifty negroes had been captured in Africa and brought to Cuba aboard a slave trader in the year 1839. Most of them were bought in the Havana slave market by two Cubans, who planned to take them by sea to plantations elsewhere on the island, aboard the coastal schooner *Amistad.* Aboard ship the Africans rebelled, killed most of the crew, and spared the two owners only on promise that they would return them to Africa. In the daylight hours, the owners steered the ship toward the Dark Continent. At night they changed course and steered toward America, until they came to Long Island and were captured.

On capture, the slave owners wanted to return the ship and cargo to Cuba. The captain of the brig wanted both, under the laws of salvage. The Spanish Minister to the United States wanted the slaves returned to Havana for trial for the murder of the ship's crew.

The question was extremely complicated, but the issue for the Abolitionists was that these were free Africans who had been enslaved, and who should be set free by the American government. The case made its way to the United States Supreme Court, and when it came time for the arguments to be made, John Quincy Adams accepted an invitation to argue in behalf of the negroes. His family lamented the decision, for they feared that it would bring trouble to all the Adamses. John Quincy Adams went ahead without question. It was a matter of principle for him.

On February 22, 1841 Adams began his argument. It was interrupted by the death of one of the Supreme Court justices, but in March the case was resumed. Adams argued that the fugitive slave laws of the United States, under which officials were obligated to return to the owner any escaped slave, could not possibly apply in international trade because by treaty the slave trade had been outlawed years before. Adams argued for some seven hours in all, and his speech was so effective that he won the case. John Quincy Adams, constantly worried about his financial affairs, presented no bill. He had taken the case as a matter of principle, and there it rested.

His success in the *Amistad* case made Adams a target in Congress for the slave-state members. Adams continued his struggle against the Gag Rule, against fighting on principle, the principle of freedom of speech, the freedom of citizens to petition the government to right wrongs, freedom of debate, and freedom of the press. In each session of Congress, Adams presented petitions relative to abolition of slavery, and sought the downfall of the Gag Rule. Each Congress voted him down, even that of 1841, when he was supported in the first vote on the matter, but defeated finally in a close contest. Had not thirty northern members of Congress voted for the Gag Rule it would have been defeated, and Congress could again have claimed to have been representative of the people of America. As it stood—and this was one of Adams' major points—all those who detested slavery were arbitrarily stilled by a Congress that protected the interest of a minority of slave-holders.

Adams was not an Abolitionist, but the fierce opposition of the South and the stubborn refusal of his fellow Congress-

men to right the wrong it committed in the Gag Rule was
driving Adams closer to the Abolitionists. The leaders of
the Abolition movement that Adams met in Washington
were a queer group. Many of them were fanatics, and their
fanaticism did not stop with Abolition. A good many combined their efforts for Abolition with efforts for Prohibi-
tion. Some were vegetarians. Others embraced other fads in
food and dress. They were allies, but allies that the wine-
loving John Quincy Adams, although basically a temperate
man, could not look upon without a feeling of mild distaste.

Adams' struggle with the southern bloc in Congress grew
ever more personal. In 1842, there came to his attention a
petition seeking his ouster as Chairman of the House Committee on Foreign Affairs, on the basis that he was so mania-
cal on the subject of color he had no right to be involved
in government relations with other nations—particularly
Mexico. Here Adams saw a chance to speak again on the
question of Gag Rule, so he tried to take the matter before
the House. In harsh debate he was again refused the right
to complete his defense. Thereafter five southern members
of the House Committee on Foreign Affairs resigned rather
than serve under him. They were replaced with other southerners, but the feeling against Adams grew more powerful
in the South with each new outbreak. Nor was the feeling
confined to the South, and to members of the opposition
Democratic party. Nominally John Quincy Adams was a
Whig—he had been supported by Whigs and Anti-Masons
in his district. But the support was in name only; Adams,
the self-styled "man of all the people" never took any party
very seriously. So when the southerners set out to try to
wreck him, the combination included southern Whigs and
northern Whigs and Democrats from everywhere.

The way to ruin Adams, his enemies decided, was to persuade the House of Representatives to vote "censure"

against him. Censure was no physical penalty. It meant that
his colleagues found his conduct objectionable and unbe-
coming to a member of the Congress. Actually, it could
mean much more. Were the disgrace itself not enough,
quite probably the man censured would not be returned
again by his constituents, for the fact of censure gave political opponents a powerful weapon. And were he returned, the object of censure would be regarded by his
fellows in the Congress as an outcast.

This was the fate planned for John Quincy Adams, sixth
President of the United States.

In January, 1842, Adams presented a petition from several Massachusetts citizens, asking for immediate dissolution of the Union of the states. Adams' reason for presenting
it was simple: he believed all petitioners had a right to be
heard and to receive answers to their petitions. But the
southerners in the House chose to make a fight on this
issue. They tried to indicate that Adams was in favor of
dissolution of the Union, and called for his censure for
bringing so improper a measure before the House.

John Quincy Adams welcomed the fight, and when one
member tried to avoid it by moving for adjournment, he
protested and won his protest against adjournment. Then
the fight began.

Adams' enemies accused him of treason, of attempting
to destroy the Union. Not so, said the old man, the issue
was the right of petition of the whole people of the Union.
If that basic right could be abridged, then there was no
freedom in America.

On the floor of the House he demanded the reading of
the Declaration of Independence—the document his father
had helped to draw. He pointed to the words. ". . . if there is
a principle sacred on earth and established by the instrument just read, it is the right of the people to alter, to

change, to destroy, the government if it become oppressive
to them . . ." There would be no such right if the people
did not have the power to petition for redress of wrong.
So said John Quincy Adams, and he rested the petition he
had just offered on the Declaration of Independence.

Adams then came under attack. Fortunately one of his
attackers spent two full days in his speech against Adams,
which gave the old man time to prepare new ammunition.
He used it well. When he began to speak, he had material
enough to continue for many days, stopping only for the
important business of the House.

As Adams began to defend himself the issue became
clear to the people in the North and West of the nation.
Petitions began to come into Congress from the entire
North, in support of Adams, and against the censure move.
The newspapers of the North took up the case and made it
famous in the struggle for constitutional rights of the people. The Whigs became uneasy, then downright troubled,
and squirmed to get out of the fight. Adams gave them their
chance, on February 7. He noted that it would take him
another week to make his defense, but if they wanted to
table the motion to censure, and would never take it up
again, he would be satisfied and stop talking. They took the
motion gratefully, and voted it, by 106 to 93—the 93 representing Democrats and southerners.

Adams' victory had several immediate results. For one
thing it brought new threats against his life by southerners.
It brought outright support of his views—although he did
not support theirs—by the radical Abolitionists in Massachusetts and elsewhere. At an Abolitionist meeting in
Faneuil Hall in Boston Adams was lionized as he had not
been since he achieved the Presidency, much in the manner
reserved for another generation of statesmen, those men
like his father who had brought the Republic into being.

In later years men who had been his enemies in this struggle—southerners—recalled that John Quincy Adams had seen the course the struggle would take in the years to come, although it is doubtful if he realized how quickly after his death the Union would fall into the final crisis that led to civil war.

Adams did not want slavery abolished in the District of Columbia, for he saw it there as a sore that festered in public. There, in the District, where Congress had the direct right to make the best life for all the people of the land, the governors of the nation permitted an abomination. He wanted to retain slavery in the District as a point of agitation —agitation which would eventually shake and destroy slavery as the slave men fought every move to restrict their "property rights."

In the debate over Adams' censure, the essential conflict of the southern position with the principles on which America had been founded was brought into sharp focus. Henry Wise, a Virginia Congressman, trying to defend slavery, declared:

"The principle of slavery is a leveling principle; it is friendly to equality. Break down slavery, and you would with the same blow destroy the great democratic principle of equality among men."

Wise actually said those words, and somehow, through the tortured logic of the white southerner who believed the black man was not a man but an animal, he believed those words.

When he said them, many members of the House at least had the good grace to laugh.

Adams did not laugh. He never laughed when engaged in combat. But he won the combat, and then he could afford to be generous. He resumed relations with those who had attacked him, but he never lost sight of the end he sought

—the end of the Gag Rule which limited freedom of speech and freedom of petition in Congress.

John Quincy Adams achieved that end during the opening session of the Twenty-eighth Congress. He introduced a resolution to kill the Gag Rule and it was adopted by a vote of 105 to 80. It came on December 3, 1844, a day John Quincy Adams commemorated in his diary by writing "blessed, ever blessed be the name of God."

Adams went on in Congress to oppose the war with Mexico and the annexation of Texas. He did not want Texas with slavery or without the agreement of Mexico (which still claimed the territory) that the United States might annex the republic. He opposed annexation of Texas but he agreed with James K. Polk that the United States should have Oregon, and he was willing to fight Britain for the Northwest Territory. When war with Mexico came, Adams supported the war effort but also supported all the efforts made to bring the war to a speedy conclusion by negotiation. He did not speak on the subject; he was growing too old and tired to speak on many subjects in the House. He had many interests, among them the Smithsonian Institution which he helped to found as a national scientific organization. He continued his own interests in various sciences, astronomy, botany, and others, and biographer Samuel Flagg Bemis said that with the exception of Benjamin Franklin, no other prominent American had done so much to promote science in America.

But in 1848, John Quincy Adams was growing tired. He suffered a cerebral hemorrhage in 1846, and while he recovered full use of his body, he wrote in his diary that he considered himself "dead" from that moment on. It was a hasty judgment, and one he might have regretted, for in one way this next year was to be his finest. When the old man, slightly tottering, walked into the House of Representatives on the morning of February 13, 1847, the members all rose to greet him, and two of his brother congressmen conducted him to his seat. John Quincy Adams, frail, and his face weathered in cottony hair and sideburns, was no longer called the Madman of Massachusetts, even by his southern adversaries. He was Old Man Eloquent to all of them. He was too weak to undertake his normal duties, and was relieved of all except the committee that supervised the Library of Congress, but he went to the sessions of the House regularly and voted in the roll calls. He was, in a way, a link between two distinct periods of American history, and the only such link. He sat in Congress with Abraham Lincoln, an undistinguished member from Illinois, and he had sat in other rooms with George Washington, and walked through the parks of Paris with Thomas Jefferson. Suddenly, it seemed, the entire nation realized that this man who had achieved more than the four score of years was a heroic figure, a symbol of the greatness of the United States.

In February, 1848, John Quincy Adams seemed much the same as usual, frail and waxen, but still active in pursuit of his varied interests. He went to the library committee meeting on February 18. The next evening he held open house for visitors. On Sunday he went to church twice, and on Monday he rode to the Capitol as usual in his carriage. He stopped to talk to others, and went to his seat early in time for the session.

Under consideration that day were decorations for several generals for actions in the campaign against Mexico. John Quincy Adams wanted to vote against those decorations—he felt strongly against the romanticizing of that "unrighteous war." He did not have a chance to vote, for before the roll was called, as the clerk was reading the citations, John Quincy Adams slumped in his seat.

When the news that John Quincy Adams was dying spread through the Capitol, the day's business was brought to an end. He was taken to the Speaker's room, where he revived enough to call for Henry Clay and to grasp that weeping Senator's hand.

"This is the end of earth, but I am composed," said the old man. Before his wife Louisa could arrive he sank into unconsciousness. He lingered thus until the evening of February 23, 1848. At twenty minutes past seven John Quincy Adams died. The link between George Washington's America and that of Abraham Lincoln was broken. The conscience of Congress, the man who reminded all of the meanings of the words written by his father and his friends, was gone. The man who dedicated his life to liberty and union, to national interest above all sectional interest— he was no more. The nation would have to find its own way.

INDEX

SELECTED BIBLIOGRAPHY

Adams, Charles Francis. (ed.) *Memoirs of John Quincy Adams*. Philadelphia: J. B. Lippincott and Co., 1874.

Bemis, Samuel Flagg. *John Quincy Adams and the Foundations of American Foreign Policy*. New York: Alfred A. Knopf, 1956.

Bemis, Samuel Flagg. *John Quincy Adams and the Union*. New York: Alfred A. Knopf, 1956.

Bishop, Joseph Bucklin. *Presidential Nominations and Elections*. New York: Charles Scribner's Sons, 1916.

Bobb, Dorothie. *Mr. and Mrs. John Quincy Adams, an Adventure in Patriotism*. New York: Minton, Balch and Co., 1930.

Bruce, Harold R. *American Parties and Politics*. New York: Henry Holt and Co., 1937.

Clark, Bennett Champ. *John Quincy Adams, Old Man Eloquent*. Boston: Little Brown and Co., 1932.

Fitzpatrick, John C. (ed.) *The Autobiography of Martin Van Buren*. Washington: Government Printing Office, 1920.

James, Marquis. *The Life of Andrew Jackson*. Indianapolis: The Bobbs Merrill Company, 1938.

Lipsky, George A. *John Quincy Adams, His Theory and Ideas*. New York: Thomas Y. Crowell, Co., 1950.

Minor, Henry. *The Story of the Democratic Party*, New York: The Macmillan Co., 1928.

Nevins, Allen (ed.) *The Diary of John Quincy Adams 1794-1845*. New York: Longmans Green and Co., 1928.

Quincy, Josiah. *Memoir of the Life of John Quincy Adams*. Boston: Phillips, Sampson, and Co., 1858.

Seward, William Henry. *Life and Public Service of John Quincy Adams*. New York: Derby, Miller, and Co., 1849.